PRACTICE
IN
TEXTUAL ANALYSIS

Appreciating Poetry

by

DR. SUSAN MACDONALD

ISBN 0 7169 3223 7

ROBERT GIBSON · Publisher
17 Fitzroy Place, Glasgow, G3 7SF, Scotland, U.K.

CONTENTS

INTRODUCTION

This book is designed to give pupils the opportunity to understand and enjoy poetry by improving their skills at textual analysis. Each poem is an exercise in close reading, in applying critical skills and in responding to the ideas presented by the poet. There should come a moment in the analysis of each poem when the pupil feels that he or she has "cracked it". He may not have an "answer" — the best poetry seldom gives us solutions; however, he will have an awareness of what the poet is writing about and he will have his own response both to the subject matter and to the way in which the poet has presented his ideas.

On another level, the book should be useful in helping pupils to sharpen their skills of textual analysis for the compulsory part of the Higher Still course. There is a need for a collection of poems or exercises that simply allow a candidate to practise for the examination.

Some poems are more accessible than others. The ones using animals as their central image — *Sparrow*, *Ringed Plover by the Water's Edge*, *The Thought-Fox* and perhaps *Sandpiper* — might be more immediately understandable than others. The "war poems" are not the usual ones: *Range-finding*, *An Irish Airman Foresees His Death* and *War Is Kind*. A few of the poems deal with family relationships, such as *The Way My Mother Speaks* and *Boy Driving His Father to Confession*. Some, like *Revelation* and *Men from the Boys*, are about growing up. In four of the poems, the form is a key to unlocking the ideas: the Shakespearean sonnets and *One Art* in particular. A couple require the pupil to detect a tongue-in-cheek tone. A few from past Higher examination papers have been included because they are worthwhile exercises which have been little used in the past when practical criticism was not compulsory. Their inclusion shows that any of these exercises from past papers could be readily adapted to the new format of Higher Still.

HOW TO USE THIS BOOK

The poems are grouped into chapters, each chapter focusing mainly on one technique, such as imagery, point of view, tone and form. The pupil should take notes or annotate the poem thoroughly before beginning the questions. The questions that accompany each poem are designed to help in the analysis. They focus on key techniques and ideas which should lead, finally, to a satisfying understanding of what the poem is really about. The answer that the pupil provides for the final question should show an overall understanding of the poem. This, surely, is what matters most: that understanding of ideas and appreciation of techniques is demonstrated. Questions are a means to an end.

These final questions also invite a reaction from the reader — real practical criticism. Did he like the ideas? Did he understand all parts of the poem? Were certain images less successful than others? In other words, this final question allows the pupil to think and to give a personal response or appreciation. It might even be beneficial occasionally to attempt the final evaluation question first — before the focused, small questions have directed consideration of the poem. In that way the pupil might come to the essay with more of his own original ideas.

Pupils have become accustomed in other subjects to using books in their own time with worked solutions for practice. Such an approach could have benefits in English and so the poems are annotated at the end of the chapter. Pupils should compare their own notes with those given. Initially, the pupil's jottings may be sparse compared to those in the book, but this is an area where practice can lead to improvement. A glossary is provided for clarification of any of the terms used in the annotations or the essays.

Accompanying each poem is a commentary or "critical appreciation". These short essays highlight some of the aspects which could be commented on in the answers to the questions; they also give a sense of the poem as a whole. Finally, they may remind us that, in the first instance, we are aiming to appreciate poetry and the ideas expressed through poems; success in examinations will usually follow this first aim as a matter of course — with practice.

When pupils are taking notes on a poem, they might remember the phrase, "WORDS FIRST":

WORD CHOICE

F	FORM
I	IMAGES
R	RHYME AND RHYTHM
S	SENTENCE STRUCTURES AND SOUND
T	TONE

These features are worth looking for in any poem. The "words" will always be there and should be looked at first. As a pupil becomes more skilled, the other techniques are worth considering in note-taking and analysis.

CHAPTER 1

Understanding the Main Ideas through Comparisons

In this chapter, four poems are offered: *Sparrow, Ringed Plover by the Water's Edge, Sandpiper* and *The Thought Fox*. In each of them a bird or animal has been the focus of the poet's attention. The considerable detail given in the poem should help you to picture the creature being described: its appearance, its movements, its habits, its habitats . . . You should look particularly at the words and phrases used in descriptions. As you read through a poem, make jottings about any particular words which strike you as especially visual or interesting or unusual or even puzzling.

After taking some notes on a poem, ask yourself if the poet could be making a comparison between the creature he describes and a type of person. In other words, is his theme a comment upon human characteristics?

The final question in the exercise, a question on evaluation of the ideas and the poetic techniques in the whole poem, allows you to write at length about what you have come to understand about the comparison the poet is making between the animal and mankind.

SPARROW

He's no artist.
His taste in clothes is more
dowdy than gaudy.
And his nest — that blackbird, writing
5   pretty scrolls on the air with the gold nib of his beak,
would call it a slum.

To stalk solitary on lawns,
to sing solitary in midnight trees,
to glide solitary over grey Atlantics —
10   not for him: he'd rather
a punch-up in a gutter.

He carries what learning he has
lightly — it is, in fact, based only
on the usefulness whose result
15   is survival. A proletarian bird.
No scholar.

But when winter soft-shoes in
and these other birds —
ballet dancers, musicians, architects —
20   die in the snow
and freeze to branches,
watch him happily flying
on the O-levels and A-levels
of the air.

Norman MacCaig

Understanding and Analysis

(a)   (i)   Explain in your own words three of the ways in which the sparrow is shown to be ordinary in the first verse (lines 1–6).   **3**

          (ii)   Show how effective you find the language of verse one in establishing a contrast between the blackbird and the sparrow. Comment on particular words or images.   **4**

(b)   (i)   What characteristic of the sparrow is conveyed by "he'd rather . . . a punch-up in the gutter." (lines 10 and 11)?   **1**

          (ii)   In what way do the first four lines of verse two (lines 7–10) present characteristics of a different type of bird from the sparrow?   **2**

         (iii)   Show how the poet emphasises these contrasts. You should consider such features as sentence structures, punctuation and word choice throughout the second verse.   **4**

(c)   (i)   How does the positioning of "lightly" (line 13) help to reinforce the meaning of the first seven words of this third verse?   **2**

          (ii)   Show how any two of the following from the third verse (lines 12–16) help to reinforce the idea that the sparrow is practical:

                sentence structure   verse structure   word choice   **4**

Evaluation

(d)   Explain fully the effect of "But" (line 17) in the development of the ideas of the poem as a whole. You should explain what ideas MacCaig conveys to you throughout the poem in the way that he gives human characteristics to the sparrow. Take into consideration the way in which language features such as word choice, imagery, structure, sound and tone, particularly in this final verse, help you to understand ideas.   **10**

                                                                        (30)

RINGED PLOVER BY THE WATER'S EDGE

They sprint eight feet and —
stop. Like that. They
sprintayard (like that) and
stop.

5   They have no acceleration
and no brakes.
Top speed's their only one.

They're alive — put life
through a burning-glass, they're
10   its focus — but they share
the world of delicate clockwork.

In spasmodic
Indian file
they parallel the parallel ripples.

15   When they stop
they, suddenly,
are gravel.

Norman MacCaig

Understanding and Analysis

(a) (i) Explain how the author uses sentence structure in the first four lines to create an impression of the ringed plover's movements. **2**

(ii) Suggest another way in which the poet reinforces the impression of the bird's movements in these lines (lines 1–4). **2**

(b) Comment on the implications of each of the words:
"share" in line 10 and "world" in line 11. **2**

(c) What does each of the words — "spasmodic" in line 12 and "Indian file" in line 13 — suggest to you about these birds? **2**

(d) By referring to the final verse (lines 15–17), show how the poet emphasises the idea of stopping. **3**

(e) (i) A "burning-glass" (line 9) is a magnifying glass. What does this idea convey to you about the ringed plover? **1**

(ii) Focusing and seeing — near and far — is a central idea of this poem and important in the overall development.
Trace the idea of seeing throughout each verse and try to reach some conclusions about what the poet is suggesting to you. **8**

Evaluation

(f) The phrase "the world of delicate clockwork" (line 11) suggests something man-made and possibly more complex than the world of the ringed plover. Does the poem suggest to you any ideas about mankind?
You should think about the ways in which the poet conveys ideas about man through his detailed description of the ringed plover throughout the poem. **10**

(30)

SANDPIPER

The roaring alongside he takes for granted,
and that every so often the world is bound to shake.
He runs, he runs to the south, finical*, awkward,
in a state of controlled panic, a student of Blake†.

5   The beach hisses like fat. On his left, a sheet
of interrupting water comes and goes
and glazes over his dark and brittle feet.
He runs, he runs straight through it, watching his toes.

    — Watching, rather, the spaces of sand between them,
10   where (no detail too small) the Atlantic drains
rapidly backwards and downwards. As he runs,
he stares at the dragging grains.

The world is a mist. And then the world is
minute and vast and clear. The tide
15   is higher or lower. He couldn't tell you which.
His beak is focussed; he is preoccupied,

looking for something, something, something.
Poor bird, he is obsessed!
The millions of grains are black, white, tan, and gray,
20   mixed with quartz grains, rose and amethyst.

Elizabeth Bishop

---

*   finical — an archaic word meaning finicky or over-particular.

†   Blake — a reference to the Romantic poet William Blake who wrote that it is possible to see "a world in a grain of sand".

Understanding and Analysis

(a)   (i)   What causes "roaring" (line 1) and the world shaking "every so often" (line 2)?   2

      (ii)   How is repetition and oxymoron used in lines 3 and 4 to show the sandpiper's attitude to his environment?   4

(b)   Comment fully on the description of the sea given in any three of these phrases:

"The beach hisses like fat" (line 5);
"a sheet of interrupting water" (lines 5 and 6);
"glazes" (line 7);
"dragging grains" (line 12).   6

(c)   Explain fully how verses two and three are linked.   4

(d)   Explain two of the contradictions contained in verse four (lines 13–16).   4

Evaluation

(e)   Elizabeth Bishop has said that the sandpiper describes herself. In what ways might a person be said to resemble the sandpiper?

Answer fully, making specific reference to the poem. The last verse (lines 17–20) might be particularly helpful in forming your ideas if you examine such language features as word choice, sentence structures, rhyme; consider too the overall structure of the poem.   10

(30)

THE THOUGHT-FOX

I imagine this midnight moment's forest:
Something else is alive
Beside the clock's loneliness
And this blank page where my fingers move.

5   Through the window I see no star:
Something more near
Though deeper within darkness
Is entering the loneliness:

Cold, delicately as the dark snow
10   A fox's nose touches twig, leaf;
Two eyes serve a movement, that now
And again now, and now, and now

Sets neat prints into the snow
Between trees, and warily a lame
15   Shadow lags by stump and in hollow
Of a body that is bold to come

Across clearings, an eye,
A widening deepening greenness,
Brilliantly, concentratedly,
20   Coming about its own business

Till, with a sudden sharp hot stink of fox
It enters the dark hole of the head.
The window is starless still; the clock ticks,
The page is printed.

Ted Hughes

Understanding and Analysis

(a)   Explain how two details in the first verse (lines 1–4) help you picture the scene.   **2**

(b)   The poet uses the same sentence structure in verses one and two. Explain how the construction helps to reflect the meaning in each instance.   **4**

(c)   (i)   How does the word choice in lines 9 and 10 help to picture the fox?   **2**

         (ii)   How does the sentence structure of lines 11 and 12 help you to imagine the fox's movements?   **2**

(d)   Go on to show fully how the fox is pictured in more detail in verses 4 and 5 (lines 13–20). You should consider such features as word choice, sentence structure, images, sound . . .   **6**

(e)   The word "till" (line 21) has a dramatic effect at that point in the poem. By looking at the words and images in the final verse, explain how these lines are a sort of climax to the poem.   **4**

Evaluation

(f)   In Hughes' "animal poems" he writes descriptively about the animals and makes them seem real. He also leads you to think that he is not only talking about the animals but about man as well.

        By referring closely to the words and images in *The Thought-fox*, explain how effective you think Hughes is at both these tasks: picturing a fox and its movements and presenting ideas about mankind.   **10**

(30)

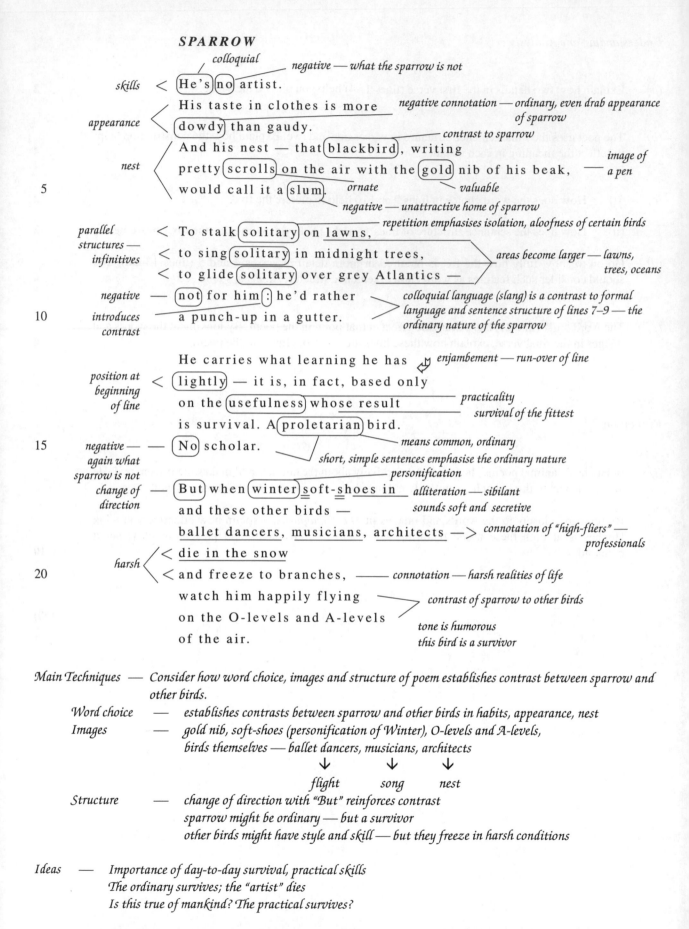

SPARROW

skills — colloquial / negative — what the sparrow is not
He's no artist.

appearance — His taste in clothes is more dowdy than gaudy.
negative connotation — ordinary, even drab appearance of sparrow

nest — And his nest — that blackbird, writing
5 pretty scrolls on the air with the gold nib of his beak,
would call it a slum.
contrast to sparrow
image of a pen
ornate — valuable
negative — unattractive home of sparrow

parallel structures — infinitives
To stalk solitary on lawns,
to sing solitary in midnight trees,
to glide solitary over grey Atlantics —
repetition emphasises isolation, aloofness of certain birds
areas become larger — lawns, trees, oceans

negative — not for him: he'd rather
10 **introduces contrast** — a punch-up in a gutter.
colloquial language (slang) is a contrast to formal language and sentence structure of lines 7–9 — the ordinary nature of the sparrow

He carries what learning he has
enjambement — run-over of line
position at beginning of line — lightly — it is, in fact, based only
on the usefulness whose result
is survival. A proletarian bird.
practicality
survival of the fittest

15 **negative — again what sparrow is not** — No scholar.
means common, ordinary
short, simple sentences emphasise the ordinary nature

change of direction — But when winter soft-shoes in
and these other birds —
personification
alliteration — sibilant sounds soft and secretive
ballet dancers, musicians, architects —
connotation of "high-fliers" — professionals

harsh — die in the snow
20 and freeze to branches,
connotation — harsh realities of life
watch him happily flying
on the O-levels and A-levels
of the air.
contrast of sparrow to other birds
tone is humorous
this bird is a survivor

Main Techniques — Consider how word choice, images and structure of poem establishes contrast between sparrow and other birds.

Word choice — establishes contrasts between sparrow and other birds in habits, appearance, nest

Images — gold nib, soft-shoes (personification of Winter), O-levels and A-levels, birds themselves — ballet dancers, musicians, architects

↓ ↓ ↓
flight song nest

Structure — change of direction with "But" reinforces contrast
sparrow might be ordinary — but a survivor
other birds might have style and skill — but they freeze in harsh conditions

Ideas — Importance of day-to-day survival, practical skills
The ordinary survives; the "artist" dies
Is this true of mankind? The practical survives?

16

Sparrow begins by making the bird seem insignificant. Words like "dowdy" and "slum" suggest that there is nothing noteworthy or creative about the sparrow's plumage or nesting habits. The poet continues to emphasise the ordinary nature of the sparrow in the colloquial language that one of this type might use: "a punch-up in the gutter". By contrast, the blackbird demands attention in his writing in the air; the words "pretty scrolls" and the image of the "gold nib" of a pen (beak) suggest ornate writing which is attractive.

This slang contrasts to the formality of the first three lines of stanza two in the repeated structure of "to stalk", "to sing" and "to glide". Each of these infinitives emphasises the isolation of grander birds who cover spaces which grow increasingly larger — from lawns to trees to "grey Atlantics". The poet suggests that the sparrow economises in what he knows — keeping with him only what is useful for day-to-day survival. The position of the word "lightly" at the beginning of line thirteen emphasises this quality and "proletarian" reinforces the idea that the sparrow is common, one of the masses. Finally, the short negative phrase "No scholar" at the end of stanza three leaves the reader in no doubt about the absence of academic achievement in the bird. The brevity of this phrase and its position at this point in the poem summarises what has been expressed in the first three stanzas and harkens back to the first line: the sparrow is "no artist" but it is ordinary in its appearance, its way of life and its accomplishments.

However, the word "but" signals a change in the direction and ideas of the poem. Once again, the poet invites us to compare the sparrow to other more accomplished birds — artists of air and space, "ballet dancers, musicians, architects". These birds can charm by their flight, by their songs and even by the way they construct their nests. The personification of winter as a secret enemy, emphasised in the sibilant sounds of words "soft-shoes", introduces the element of danger. The sinister and sudden appearance of winter is followed by words with bleak connotations. The pictures of birds dying in the snow or, even more dramatically, freezing to death on branches reminds us that the practical skills of survival have their own value.

The poet ends on a lighter note with the sparrow, again in contrast to other birds, surviving happily in the testing times of winter. The "O-levels and A-levels of the air", as well as earlier expressions like "punch-up in the gutter" and "proletarian bird", and even some of the exaggerated contrasts, remind us that the tone here is a bit tongue-in-cheek. The poet is not offering us a serious lesson to take to heart; just a suggestion that maybe some practical skills are as important at the end of the day as aesthetic, creative, scholastic accomplishments. After all, daily survival is the essential ingredient for life before we begin decorating our existence with scrolls and songs.

RINGED PLOVER BY THE WATER'S EDGE

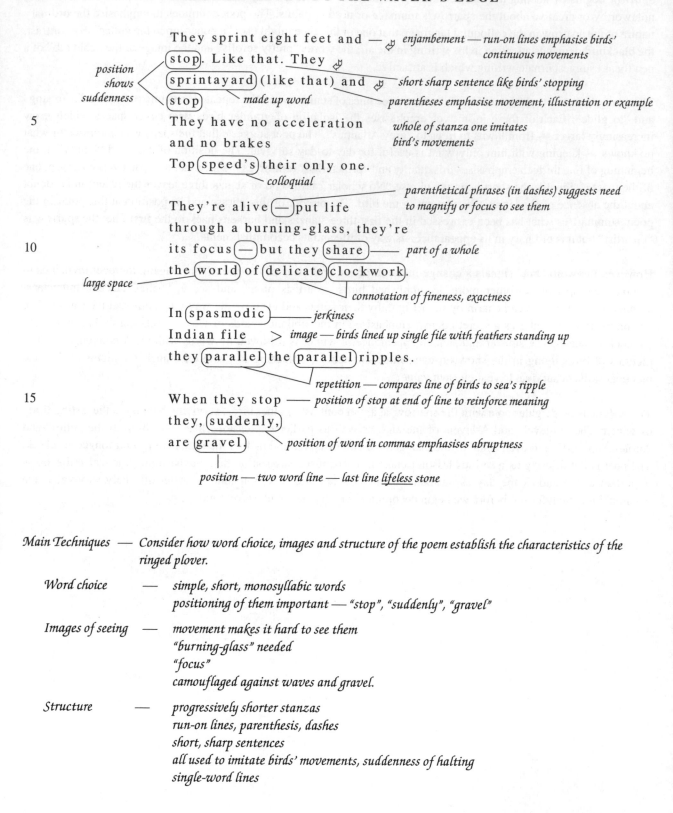

They sprint eight feet and —   *enjambement — run-on lines emphasise birds'*
                                                   continuous movements

position
shows
suddenness

stop. Like that. They

sprintayard (like that) and   *short sharp sentence like birds' stopping*

stop   *made up word*   *parentheses emphasise movement, illustration or example*

5   They have no acceleration   *whole of stanza one imitates*
and no brakes   *bird's movements*

Top speed's their only one.
       colloquial

They're alive — put life   *parenthetical phrases (in dashes) suggests need*
                                               to magnify or focus to see them
through a burning-glass, they're

10   its focus — but they share — *part of a whole*

the world of delicate clockwork.

large space   *connotation of fineness, exactness*

In spasmodic   *jerkiness*

Indian file   > *image — birds lined up single file with feathers standing up*

they parallel the parallel ripples.

                     repetition — compares line of birds to sea's ripple

15   When they stop — *position of stop at end of line to reinforce meaning*

they, suddenly,

are gravel.   *position of word in commas emphasises abruptness*

position — two word line — last line lifeless *stone*

Main Techniques — *Consider how word choice, images and structure of the poem establish the characteristics of the ringed plover.*

   Word choice — *simple, short, monosyllabic words*
      positioning of them important — "stop", "suddenly", "gravel"

   Images of seeing — *movement makes it hard to see them*
      "burning-glass" needed
      "focus"
      camouflaged against waves and gravel.

   Structure — *progressively shorter stanzas*
      run-on lines, parenthesis, dashes
      short, sharp sentences
      all used to imitate birds' movements, suddenness of halting
      single-word lines

   Ideas — *Birds are part of whole — "the world of delicate clockwork" — difficulty in seeing them individually.*
      Is the ringed plover like man? Difficulty of concentrating on the individual.

In the previous poem, *Sparrow*, MacCaig uses a bird to suggest general ideas about man. He uses the same technique in the poem *Ringed Plover by the Water's Edge*. First he establishes a detailed picture of the ringed plover, particularly its rapid, quick-fire movements. The first sentence is a short simple sentence. The second statement is not even a sentence. Words like "sprint" contrast to "stop" and suggest the jerkiness of the birds' movements. The extremes of actions are further suggested by "no acceleration and no brakes". The run-on lines (enjambement) of the first stanzas reinforce the suddenness of their stopping. Twice the single, simple, monosyllabic word "stop" is on a line by itself. He further shows the speed of movement with a humorous touch in the word he makes up — "sprintayard" — and in the parenthetical phrase that follows — "(like that)" — just in case we had missed the idea that he is imitating the bird's movements by these language features. The idea of magnification or "burning-glass" suggests that the birds are difficult to bring into focus, possibly because of size and also speed.

In the middle of the second stanza initiated by the word "but", the poet begins to draw our attention away from the close focus we have had on the ringed plover. "Share" and "world" suggest that we need to see the plover against a greater scene. The phrase "delicate clockwork" particularly suggests a world where the smallest of parts and the most delicate creations work in harmony to keep things moving. The ringed plover is only one small part of the whole. When we move back to looking at the plovers, it is to see them lined up single-file like Indians against the larger background of the sea. The repetition of the word "parallel" emphasises the idea of a line — in the line of plovers and in a long wave.

The final verse again shows how difficult it is to keep the small part in focus: when the ringed plovers stop, they disappear. They are camouflaged against the gravel and they become part of the larger scene, impossible to depict without their distinctive jerky — "spasmodic" — movements. The suddenness of their stopping and disappearance is emphasised by the positioning of the word "suddenly" between the subject and the verb and also by the form of the stanza with "gravel" in the final line. MacCaig develops this visual idea from the first stanza when they all run as one and are therefore difficult to distinguish; the burning-glass in the second stanza emphasises the difficulty of keeping in focus something which is so small and fast; in the third stanza they blend into their background — "they parallel the parallel ripples".

MacCaig is suggesting to me that even the smallest creature is part of a whole, a world that works like "delicate clockwork". It is difficult to see the smallest of the parts against the whole — they run parallel to or are camouflaged against the larger features — but they nevertheless are significant in the overall creation. The poem is a visual one which tries to help the reader to focus on the small and the large, the near and the far.

SANDPIPER

huge sound of sea

The (roaring) alongside he takes for granted, *a*
    huge movement

and that (every so often) the world is bound to (shake.) *b*

the surf

He runs, he runs to the south, finical, awkward, *c*

in a state of controlled panic, a student of (Blake). *b*
    reference to grains of sand

repetition — frantic   oxymoron

5   Image — hissing, sizzling sound

(The beach hisses like fat.) On his left, a sheet *d*
    image — wave like a sheet of glass

of interrupting water comes and goes *e* *breakable*

and (glazes) over his dark and (brittle) feet. *d*

glass

He runs, he runs straight through it, (watching) his toes. *e*

repetition

dash — emphasises break

"watching" connects two stanzas — watching toes and watching space

— (Watching), rather, the spaces of sand between them, *f* *huge*

10   emphasises detail in parenthesis

where (no detail too small) the (Atlantic) (drains) *g*

rapidly backwards and downwards. As he runs, *h* *pull*

he stares at the (dragging) grains. *g*

unclear   power and pull of sea

great size — (The world) is a (mist). And then the world is *i*

presents opposite minute and vast mist and clear

(minute) (and) (vast) (and) (clear). The tide *j* *polysyndetic "and" emphasises contrasts*

15   is higher or lower. He couldn't tell you which. *k* *— opposites — higher/lower*
    — focussed/preoccupied

His beak is focussed; he is preoccupied, *j*

repetition   emphasises vagueness of goal and frantic nature of search

small letter — (l)ooking for something, something, something. *l*

unimportance suggestion of hopelessness

(Poor) bird, he is (obsessed!) — *emotive word with exclamation* *m*

The millions of grains are black, white, tan, and gray, *n*

20   mixed with quartz grains, rose and amethyst. *m*

half-rhyme in this stanza

something valuable   variety and richness of colour

Main techniques — Consider how word choice, images and structure of the poem help you see the sandpiper as a certain type of indivicual.

Word choice — to describe sea — large, powerful
to describe bird — monosyllable, simple words repeated

Imagery — hisses like fat — sound effects of surf
glass imagery — extended → glazes and brittle — idea of seeing through and idea of breaking

Structure — 3 stanzas — bird's perspective
4th stanza — change in perspective — looking at bird

Ideas — Concern with detail. Is this obsessive, short-sighted and boring or does it help us to realise the wealth and variety of the world — even the smallest of objects like a grain of sand?

Sandpiper is another poem which explores an aspect of human nature — the concentration on detail. The first three verses suggest that the sandpiper is obsessed with grains of sand. The description of the sandpiper is not complimentary: "finical" implies the over-particular; "awkward" suggests lack of elegance in movement possibly caused by near-sightedness; the oxymoron "controlled panic" implies constant fear with limited, predictable reactions. The repetition of "he runs" reinforces the limited and mindless reactions to fear.

By contrast, the description of the sea from the sandpiper's perspective conveys the hugeness in the "roaring" and in the shaking of the beach with the pounding surf. The imagery further suggests the sound of the surf "hissing like fat" and the extended glass imagery suggests transparency of the water. Strangely, these images seemed to me initially inappropriate. The phrase "like fat" is odd when the sea is cold although in terms of sound it might be a good description. Glass, while showing the transparency of the sea, is wrong in terms of texture: the sea moves and rolls; glass is inflexible and breaks. Yet these images could be appropriate from a sandpiper's perspective because it lacks real knowledge of the larger world, intense in its concentration on sand.

The repetition of "watching" linking verses two and three reinforces the unflagging concentration on the very smallest of spaces — between the sandpiper's toes. The words "drains" and "dragging" suggests that the sandpiper only feels the effects of the sea as it pulls the grains down and back from his intense near-sighted vision. We are reminded of the larger world in the short, simple sentence, "The world is a mist". The world is described in contradictions: small and large; misty and clear; the tides high and low. The sandpiper, with his focussed concentration, obsessed with grains, is unaware of what is happening around him.

The final run-on stanza with the small "l" suggests that nothing is going to happen to the sandpiper as it continues searching; repeating "something" implies that the object of the search will never be identified and that "it" is not valuable or sufficiently distinctive to merit a name. On the other hand, the final description of the sand suggests beauty, variety and even wealth (amethyst). The ending is ambiguous: the sandpiper is "poor" and "obsessed" — emotive, derogatory words; but small is beautiful. The regular rhyme scheme might suggest the rhythm of tides and surf breaking; the final half-rhyme (polysyllabic "obsessed" and "amethyst") is unsatisfactory. The sandpiper misses so much. The poet seems to be asking whether the type of perception that concentrates on richness of detail is laughable in its mindless lack of imagination and narrowness of focus.

an unusual animal

THE (THOUGHT)-FOX

Personal — *the mind — imagination* — *alliteration draws attention to time*

(I) (imagine) this midnight moment's forest:

indefinite, vague — Something else is alive

Beside the (clock's) (loneliness) — *sadness, silence*

And this (blank) page where my fingers move.

nothing to say — *ticking*

5   Through the window I see no (star) — *introduces what the poet sees through the window*

vague < Something more (near) — *does not look at the distance*

Though deeper within darkness

Is entering the loneliness:

softly, carefully

(Cold,) (delicately) as the dark snow — *odd combination*

10   A fox's (nose) touches twig, leaf; — *smallest of movements — eyes*

movements are tentative — Two eyes serve a movement, that now

And again now, and now, and now

Repetition of "now" and "and" emphasise hesitancy of movements — *enjambement also emphasises continual slow movements*

Sets neat prints into the snow ——— *"t" sound seems precise*

lack of reality — Between trees, and warily a lame — *shows hesitancy*

15   (Shadow) (lags) by stump and in hollow

slow movement — hangs back — Of a body that is bold to come — *enjambement reinforces idea of continual, slow movements*

Across clearings, an eye,

A widening deepening greenness, > *close focus on detail — the eye*

Brilliantly, concentratedly,

20   Coming about its own business

suddenness of appearance — *monosyllables* — *unpleasant connotation*

(Till,) with a sudden sharp hot (stink) of fox

It enters the dark hole of the head. — *image of hole in head — relates to title*

The window is starless still; the clock ticks,

conclusive short sentence < The page is printed. — *echo of the poem's start*

alliteration emphasises emptiness of sky

Main Techniques — Consider how word choice, images and structure help you understand what the sudden appearance of the fox represents for this poet.

     Word choice — conveying silence and isolation and sensual detail
                       repetition and sound suggesting fox's movements
     Structure — also suggesting tentative nature of fox's movements
     Images — the fox, stars/starless, the page, the title.

Ideas — The slow, tentative nature of creativity — also, not an altogether pleasant experience. And the closeness of inspiration — not in the stars (idealistic) but the fox (reality).

From the unusual title of *The Thought-Fox*, we are led to believe that Hughes is writing about an odd creature — more than a fox as we know it. Nevertheless, he uses close detailed description to picture the animal and its movements in a realistic way. The poet seems to be writing — or unable to write — "blank page" — late at night. The silence and loneliness is conveyed by the clock's ticking and the alliteration of "midnight moment" drawing attention to the time.

The fox enters this quiet scene in a stealthy, hesitant way reinforced by the parallel sentence structures used in the first two stanzas. Each stanza introduces the fox to the scene in a sentence with a colon and with the word "something" indicating mystery, uncertainty, doubt, the difficulty of seeing clearly what is about to appear. The words used to describe the fox further suggest the reluctance and tentative nature of its approach. It is the only moving object on the frozen landscape, barely making an impression on the scene as it touches objects with its nose only. The structure of the sentence with the repeated "now" and "and" also suggests this slow hesitancy of the fox — cautiously, step by step. The "t" sound in "sets neat prints" shows the delicacy, the precision, the lightness of touch and the connotation of the words "warily", "lame" and "lags" all reinforce the feeling that the fox may never fully enter the clearing but remain only a "shadow" lurking in the darkness. However, the enjambement or running on from stanza to stanza suggests that the movements continue slowly until the poet can focus on the part of the fox that seems to move most noticeably — its deep penetrating green eye which seems almost hypnotic in the description that Hughes gives it.

Finally, and almost shockingly, after its slow approach, the fox appears. The position of the word "till" at the beginning of the verse, the alliteration of "sudden, sharp", and the unpleasant connotations of "stink" make this appearance dramatic. We are left with several uncomfortable impressions although the poet has been successful in printing the page: the poet still cannot see the distance — the stars; the clock is still ticking in loneliness; and the appearance of the "fox" has not been an altogether pleasant one — sudden, hot and "stinking". However, the poet has been successful in writing something. The creative process seems to have its difficulties and its unpleasant aspects.

CHAPTER 2

Awareness of Point of View in a Poem

In this chapter, four poems show a poet adopting a voice or a "persona" to convey experiences and ideas: *Relevation, Boy Driving His Father to Confession, Men* and *The Way My Mother Speaks*. In each of these, the poet "becomes" a person; he or she tells about his experience from a personal, first-person, point of view. You should read each poem closely looking for details about the particular experience and also noticing any change or development which you can see in the central persona of the poem. You should look for words or phrases or symbols which are used to suggest that the persona is changing inwardly, in his thoughts and feelings. Make jottings about particular words which tell you something about the person or even puzzle you or seem strange.

In *Revelation*, the persona is a woman or girl remembering a time when she was younger. A visit to a farm helped her to realise things about herself and about life in general which she had not thought of before the experience.

In *Boy Driving His Father to Confession*, the persona is a man looking back at times in his youth when his relationship with his father began to alter. At these stages in his life he understands more about himself and about his father.

In *Men* the persona — a woman — is reflecting on her relationship with various types of men (generally or specifically?).

Finally, in *The Way My Mother Speaks*, a young woman is travelling away from home and her mother. She seems unable to forget her childhood.

After taking your notes on each of these poems, ask yourself if the poet could be talking about relationships or experiences which have a universal significance as well as individual or personal meaning. In using an individual's experience, is he or she expressing ideas about the way we change and mature as we grow older? Or is the poet writing about the way relationships, perhaps within a family, alter as the individuals change and mature?

The last question for each poem asks you to write at greater length about the particular experience described in the poem and to show how it might lead to general observations on human nature and changing relationships.

REVELATION

I remember once being shown the black bull
when a child at the farm for eggs and milk.
They called him Bob — as though perhaps
you could reduce a monster
5   with the charm of a friendly name.
At the threshold of his outhouse, someone
held my hand and let me peer inside.
At first, only black
And the hot reek of him. Then he was immense,
10   his edges merging with the darkness, just
a big bulk and a roar to be really scared of,
a trampling, and a clanking tense with the chain's jerk.
His eyes swivelled in the great wedge of his tossed head.
He roared his rage. His nostrils gaped.

15   And in the yard outside,
oblivious hens picked their way about.
The faint and rather festive tinkling
behind the mellow stone and hasp was all they knew
of that Black Mass, straining at his chains.
20   I had always half-known he existed —
this antidote* and Anti-Christ† his anarchy
threatening the eggs, well-rounded, self-contained —
and the placidity of milk.

I ran, my pigtails thumping alien on my back in fear,
25   past the big boys in the farm lane
who pulled the wings from butterflies and
blew up frogs with straws.
Past thorned hedge and harried nest,
scared of the eggs shattering —
30   only my small and shaking hand on the jug's rim
in case the milk should spill.

Liz Lochead

---

*   antidote — a medicine given to counteract the effects of poison.

†   Anti-Christ — the opposite, the opponent of Christ.

Understanding and Analysis

(a)   How does the poet in the first five lines convey the idea that this was a memorable experience for this young child?
You should consider how details are expressed in word choice and sentence structures.   **3**

(b)   Show how the poet increases the drama of the moment that the child sees the bull by any three of the following techniques used in lines 6–14:

      (i)   sensual description;
      (ii)   sound;
      (iii)   verb forms;
      (iv)   imagery.   **6**

(c)   (i)   What significance do you think the hens have in this poem? Think particularly about the word "oblivious" (line 16).   **2**

      (ii)   How does the word choice suggest a contrast between the hens and the bull in lines 15–23?   **2**

(d)   Eggs and milk take on symbolic significance in lines 22–31. What significance can you see in keeping with the ideas of this poem?

You may wish to look at the adjectives particularly in lines 22 and 23 in helping you to see the symbolism.   **4**

(e)   The effects of this experience on the child is central to understanding this poem. How appropriate do you find the experience conveyed in lines 24–27 in furthering your understanding of what this event meant to the child?   **3**

Evaluation

(f)   (i)   How satisfying do you find the last four lines as a conclusion to the girl's experience and as an ending for the poem in both techniques and ideas? You should consider the details of these lines and relate them to your appreciation of the poem as a whole, including the title.

      (ii)   Go on to explain how effectively you think the poet conveys this particular experience of the girl and also suggests that this is a general experience that we all encounter.   **10**

(30)

BOY DRIVING HIS FATHER TO CONFESSION

Four times now I have seen you as another
Man, a grown-up friend, less than a father;
Four times found chinks in the paternal mail*
To find you lost like me, quite vulnerable.

5   There was the time when my child brother died
And in the porch, among the men, you cried.
Again, last year, I was shocked at your tears
When my mother's plane took off. In twelve years
You had not been apart for one whole day

10   Till this long-talked-of, two-week holiday:
I left you lonely at the barrier,
Was embarrassed later when you stood a beer.
The third time you made a man of me
by telling me an almost smutty story

15   In a restaurant toilet. We both knew
This was an unprecedented breakthrough.

To-day, a sinner, and shy about it,
You asked me to drive up to church, and sit
Morose as ever, telling me to slow

20   On corners or for potholes that I know
As well as you do. What is going on
Under that thick grey skull? What confession
Are you preparing? Do you tell sins as I would?
Does the same hectic rage in our one blood?

25   Here at the churchyard I am slowing down
To meet you, the fourth time, on common ground.
You grunt, and slam the door. I watch another
Who gropes as awkwardly to know his father.

Seamus Heaney

*   mail — means armour, such as a knight might put on for protection.

(a)   (i)   Explain in your own words what the speaker is saying about his relationship with his father in lines 1 and 2.   **2**

        (ii)   By referring to the word choice, particularly "chinks" and "paternal mail", of line 3, explain what the speaker has discovered about his father.   **4**

(b)   The poet refers to "four times" (lines 1 and 3). Explain the father's emotion on the first occasion (lines 5 and 6) and his feelings the second time (lines 7–12).   **4**

(c)   (i)   How does "unprecedented breakthrough" (line 16) suggest the nature of the relationship between father and son "the third time"?   **2**

        (ii)   Choose another phrase from lines 13–16 and show how it tells you more about this relationship.   **2**

    2

(d)   How does "today" (line 17) mark a turning point in the poem?

(e)   Explain how the sentence structure of lines 21–24 helps to reveal the poet's feelings about his relationship with his father?   **2**

    2

(f)   Can you explain two meanings of the title?

Evaluation

(g)   (i)   The poem is ambiguous in a number of places. Consider the use of the word "another" in both lines 1 and 27, also the ambiguity of the title and "sinner" (line 17)? What ideas about the relationship between the father and son has this poem suggested to you? You should consider the whole poem but perhaps concentrate particularly on the events of the "fourth time" (line 26) in answering this question.

        (ii)   Go on to explain what ideas the poet suggests to you about the father/son or parent/child relationship generally.   **10**

    (30)

MEN

I like the simple sort, the soft white-collared ones
smelling of wash that someone else has done,
of apples, hard new wood. I like the thin-skinned,
outdoor, crinkled kind, the athletes, big-limbed,
5   who stoop to hear, the moneyed men, the unironic
leisured sort who balk at jokes and have to blink,
the men with houses, kids in cars, who own
the earth and love it, know themselves at home
here, and so don't know they're born, or why
10   born is hard, but snatch life smack from the sky,
a cricket ball caught clean that fills the hand.

I put them all at sea. They peer at my dark land
as if through sun on dazzling waves, and laugh.

Kate Clanchy

Understanding and Analysis

(a)   (i)   By referring to the language of the first line of the poem, show how the poet helps you to picture the type of man described.   **2**

         (ii)   What does "wash that someone else has done" (line 2) suggest about this type?   **2**

(b)   Choose three of the other types mentioned and say how the poet makes each distinctive by her use of language.   **6**

(c)   The poet suggests several times in the first eleven lines of the poem that men might not understand as much as she does. Explain how any three of the following might suggest that men do not know as much:

        (i)   "who stoop to hear" (line 5);
        (ii)   "unironic" (line 5);
        (iii)   "balk at jokes" (line 6);
        (iv)   "have to blink" (line 6);
        (v)   "don't know they're born" (line 9);
        (vi)   "why born is hard" (lines 9 and 10).   **6**

(d)   Explain how the poet uses sound in line 10 and in line 11 to reinforce the meaning.   **2**

(e)   Suggest why the poet makes a division between line 11 and line 12.   **2**

Evaluation

(f)   Study carefully the final couplet, particularly the central metaphor, and also words like "peer", "dark", "dazzling" and "laugh" and explain your overall understanding of the whole poem and the persona's relationship with men.   **10**

(30)

THE WAY MY MOTHER SPEAKS

I say her phrases to myself
in my head
or under the shallows of my breath,
restful shapes moving.
5 *The day and ever. The day and ever.*

The train this slow evening
goes down England
browsing for the right sky,
too blue swapped for a cool grey.
10 For miles I have been saying
What like is it
the way I say things when I think.
Nothing is silent. Nothing is not silent.
What like is it.

15 Only tonight
I am happy and sad
like a child
who stood at the end of summer
and dipped a net
20 in a green, erotic pond. *The day
and ever. The day and ever.*
I am homesick, free, in love
with the way my mother speaks.

Carol Ann Duffy

Understanding and Analysis

(a)   (i)   Give two reasons why the words in line 5 are in italics.   2

         (ii)   What is unusual about the phrase "restful shapes moving" (line 4)?   2

(b)   How does the poet use sentence structure and sound in lines 6–9 to draw attention to the length or
         tedium of the journey?   2

(c)   Show how the poet uses three of the following techniques in stanza two (lines 6–14) to draw
         attention to the persona's state of mind:

         (i)   repetition;
         (ii)   word choice;
         (iii) contrast;
         (iv)   contradiction.   6

(d)   In lines 15–20, an image is used to help explain what this journey means to the traveller. Explain the
         implications of that image fully.   4

(e)   Explain how the poet creates an atmosphere or mood in this poem. Think about which words
         particularly contribute to the mood.   4

Evaluation

(f)   (i)   Contradictions or paradoxes are an essential aspect of this poem. Explore the contradictions
                fully throughout the poem, showing to what extent they are effective in contributing to your
                understanding of the state of mind of the persona and ideas that the poem raises for you.

         (ii)   Go on to explain how effective you found this poem in expressing more general experience.   10

                                                                                                                                                 (30)

REVELATION — *realisation or sudden understanding*

Personal memory   *singular experience*   *passive voice*

(I) remember (once) (being shown) the b̲lack b̲ull — *alliteration draws attention to horror*

friendly connotations   when a child at the farm for eggs and milk

They called him (Bob) — as though perhaps you

could reduce a m̲onster̲ — *image of size and danger*

5   *edge*   with the charm of a friendly name

At the (threshold) of his outhouse, (someone) — *vague*

needs reassurance   h̲eld my h̲and and let me (peer inside.) — *suggests difficulty in seeing*

At first, only (black) — *evil?*

sense of smell and touch   And the (hot reek) of him. Then he was immense, > *then sight*

10   his edges merging with the darkness, just

a b̲ig b̲ulk and a (roar) to be really scared of, *sound (onomatopoeia)*

alliteration   a (trampling,) and a (clanking) tense with the chain's jerk. > *bulk is chained*

unpleasant picture   His (eyes swivelled) in the great wedge of his tossed head.

He r̲oared his r̲age. His nostrils (gaped). > *image of blood — gaped like a wound*

alliteration emphasises sound   *size*

15   And in the yard outside.

(oblivious) hens (picked their way about). > *looking at ground*

movement to outside   The f̲aint and rather f̲estive tinkling ———————— *alliteration, onomatopoeia*

capitals — importance   behind the mellow stone and hasp was all they knew *they can't see bull — can only*

vague awareness   of that (B)lack (M)ass, straining at his chains. > *hear deceptive tinkling sound of*

20   *of evil —*   I had always (half-known) he existed — *the devil/evil* *chains*

darkness   this a̲ntidote and A̲nti-Christ his a̲narchy

threatening the (eggs,) well- (rounded) , (self-contained) — *adjectives suggest wholeness, completeness, well-being*

and the placidity/of milk.

to break the eggs   *sign of youth*

running home   I ran, my (pigtails) thumping alien on my back in fear,

25   past the b̲ig b̲oys in the farm lane — *alliteration reminds us of bull and stresses this fear — boys*

who pulled the wings from butterflies and

blew up frogs with straws. ↘ *evil, cruel, savage, uncivilised actions suggesting anarchy and chaos*

return journey from farm has danger   Past (thorned) hedge and (harried) nest,

scared of the (eggs) (shattering) — *symbol — well-being*

now breaking

30   only my (small) and (shaking) hand on the jug's rim

in case the milk (should spill) *suggests vulnerability — we feel sympathy*

loss of "milk"

Main Techniques — *Consider how word choice, contrasts and symbolism help to convey this experience from a child's point of view.*

     Word choice — *sensual, vivid*

     Contrast — *between inside darkness / outside light*

           between girl's awareness / hens' oblivion

           between journey to farm / journey home

     Symbols — *eggs and milk, bull.*

Ideas — *A child trying to hold on to her wholesome childhood peace and innocence when she becomes aware of some startling aspect of the adult world — evil, sin, danger, sex?*

34

Revelation means a sudden awareness. This is an appropriate title for a poem in which a young girl is made suddenly aware of greater dangers in life through a brief but memorable experience when visiting a farm to collect eggs and milk. This awareness becomes most apparent in the last four lines of the poem. The journey to the farm for these items might be a daily occurrence but this experience — seeing a big, black bull — she remembers happening "once". The parenthetical phrase at the beginning of the poem suggests that the "friendly name" of Bob (one might expect this name in a sheep dog) was singularly inappropriate for what seemed to the child a "monster".

She remembers the details of the moment vividly. At first the bull is difficult to see in the darkness of the outbuilding; she can only"peer" into the unknown. Her sensual impressions (other than sight) are strong: she feels the heat of him; smells the "reek", a word suggesting strong, unpleasant odours; and she hears the "trampling" and the "clanking". Most memorable is the movement of his eyes — frightening, swivelling movements as the eyes roll from side to side without movement of the head. The enormity of that head is emphasised in the word "wedge". The final line of this stanza completes the frightening picture with the alliteration and onomatopoeia of "roared his rage". Most poignant of all is the description of his nostrils — flared and gaping "like wounds" — suggesting the colour of blood and a vulnerability of this enormous animal in chains.

By contrast to the girl, the silly hens are "oblivious", picking their way about the ground, able to know the bull only by the sounds they hear which to them seem "festive" and merely "faint". The awareness of the young child is greater; she had already guessed at the potential in the world for anarchy, chaos, lack of order and injustice — all the things we most fear. Yet as a very young child her security is represented by the eggs she goes to fetch — "well-rounded" and "self-contained" — and the milk. The word "placidity" suggests the peaceful calm and harmony of countryside. From this significant moment, the young child is aware that darkness and evil is always present, symbolised by the bull. As if to provide an example of this, the next stanza shows the threat — "big boys" who show such savagery as pulling wings from butterflies and blowing up frogs with straws. This horror may be considered as shocking as the darkness and immensity of the bull.

At the end of the poem, the girl who walks home down the farm lane of "thorns" and "harried" nests is different from the one who arrived to collect eggs and milk. She is aware of the fragility of eggs and the likelihood of milk to spill: her well-being is under threat now that she has become aware (*Revelation*) of that "Black Mass" (deserving of the capital letters) straining at its chains — the sound of the phrase drawing attention to the precarious state of innocence and well-being in the presence of danger and evil in the world.

BOY DRIVING HIS FATHER TO CONFESSION

youth? son? — BOY (circled)
personal
2 meanings — driving car / forcing confession

enjambement puts emphasis on "another" and "man"

Four times now I have seen you as another
Man, a grown-up friend, less than a father;   *a*
Four times found chinks in the paternal mail   *b*
To find you lost like me, quite vulnerable.   *b*

repetition
holes in armour — *armour* — *pejorative* — *fatherly* — *suggests vulnerability, weakness*

5
There was the time when my child brother died   *c*
And in the porch, (among the men,) you cried.   *c*
Again, last year, I was shocked at your tears   *d*
When my mother's plane took off. In twelve years   *d*
You had not been apart for one whole day   *e*
10
Till this long-talked-of, two-week holiday: *e*
I left you lonely at the barrier,   *f*
Was embarrassed later when you stood a beer.   *f*

① first time / father cried
commas emphasis "men"
② second time / mother's departure on holiday
lonely — vulnerable
matey relationship — not father / son

The third time you made a man of me   *g*
by telling me an almost smutty story   *g*
15
In a restaurant toilet. We both knew   *h*
This was an unprecedented breakthrough.   *h*

③ third time — acts like a mate
made a man — state of maturity
smutty — negative connotation — sleazy
never happened before
past

confession
To-day, a sinner, and shy about it,   *i*
You asked me to drive up to church, and sit   *i*
Morose as ever, telling me to slow   *j*
20
On corners or for potholes that I know   *j*
As well as you do. What is going on   *k*
Under that thick grey skull? What confession   *k*
Are you preparing? Do you tell sins as I would?   *l*
Does the same hectic rage in our one blood?   *l*

present / new stanza change in relationship? / fourth chink in armour
ambiguity — who is sinner? Father or son?
father telling him how to drive
symbol? — obstacles?
questions — doesn't understand his father
④ fourth time — going to confession
suggests confusion / are they similar?

25
Here at the churchyard I am slowing down   *m*
To meet you, the fourth time, on common ground.   *m*
You grunt, and slam the door. I watch another   *a*
Who gropes as awkwardly to know his father.   *a*

religion? / grave?
lack of communication
echoes of first two lines
uncertainty of movements

Main Techniques — Consider how word choice, contrasts and structure help you to understand this experience from a young man's point of view.
Contrast between father and son — similarities and differences. Ambiguity used — in "another" and in title
Word choice — connotations of "vulnerability" — "embarrassed" — "smutty" — "morose"
Structure — four times son sees vulnerability of father — similarities and differences on each occasion
past (first half) and present — second half (today).

Ideas — Difficulty of father / son relationship — "knowing" another who you "know" so well. Embarrassment / concern at seeing another — a father — a "hero" figure becoming increasingly vulnerable and weak.

Boy Driving His Father to Confession is about a "boy's" relationship with his father — difficult and awkward at the best of times. The simple, rhyming couplets move through four experiences of the boy (who is now an adult and the speaker of the poem). The experiences are memories of times when the son saw his father vulnerable and weak when previously he had considered him great like a knight in armour. Four times he saw "chinks" or holes in the "mail" and the father, as a grown-up friend, was a less than heroic figure.

The first occasion was the death of a younger son when the father, among other men, showed weakness and cried. The second occasion was when the mother went on holiday, separating the two for the first time in twelve years. On that occasion, the friendly parental relationship was furthered by the father when he bought his son a beer and this "matey" friendship almost embarrassed the son. The third occasion was when he told his son a "smutty story" or a "dirty" or suggestive joke in a toilet. The words "unprecedented" and "breakthrough" suggest that this type of closeness had not previously occurred.

A change comes, however, in the second stanza with the first word, "today". The fourth occasion in the present is the most significant. The first line of the second stanza is initially ambiguous: "Today, a sinner, and shy about it". Who is the "sinner" and who is "shy"? The "boy" now drives his father to the church for confession. Although the son is now old enough to drive, the father is still giving his son advice about how to miss the "potholes" which could be implying obstacles more significant than the holes in the road. The series of rhetorical questions which follow suggest that the son is confused. He does not understand his father and his motivations. Words like "grunt" and "slam" imply a lack of communication. "Gropes" and "awkwardly" also suggests that the efforts to understand — possibly on the part of both father and son — are difficult and uncertain.

The title can have two meanings: "driving" a car or forcing a confession.

The ambiguity of the final line (which echoes in its rhyme the first two lines of the poem) brings us back to the ideas of the title and the beginning. The speaker seems to be suggesting that this is a common experience — almost a ritual for father and son to fail to understand each other finally. The enjambement of the first line focuses the attention of the reader on this ambiguity of "another / Man". The sense of the final line also leaves us uncertain. Who is the speaker watching? Who is the "boy" in the title? Is this every man?

Finally, the idea of confession and sinner should be considered. The speaker is not really writing about drinking beer and telling smutty jokes but about knowing the real weaknesses and vulnerability of men: all the harder to accept when we see the weaknesses and sins in those we love the most.

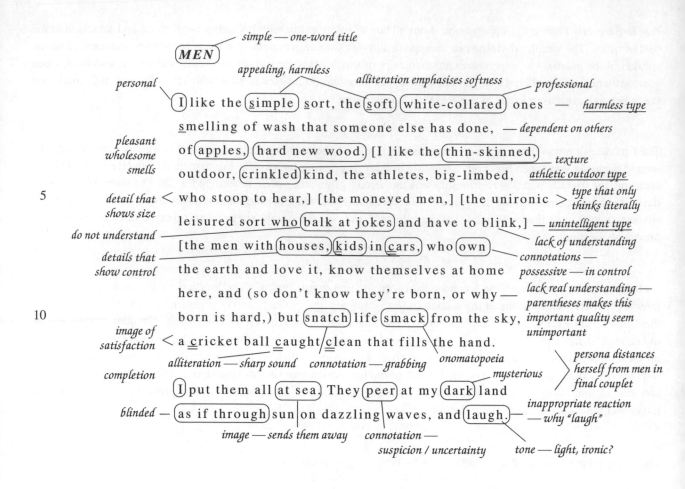

Main Techniques — Consider how word choice, imagery, sound and structure help to consider the poet/persona's relationship with men.

Structure — thirteen (unlucky) line poem is unusual
eleven lines giving details of variety of types of men
final couplet — uses extended metaphor of sea and land.

Word choice — details that have strong positive and negative connotations
details well chosen to convey types of men

Imagery — extended metaphor — poet is "dark land" — mysterious
men are "at sea" about her — blinded, lack understanding

Sound — rhyme — half rhyme throughout — never quite satisfying. Couplet connected to main part by rhyme (hand / land)

alliteration —
onomatopoeia — > to help portray types

Idea — Exploration of relationship with different types of men. Making fun ("laugh") of various characteristics of men that show simplicity and lack of understanding.

38

In *Men* the poet seems to be exploring in a humorous way her relationship with men generally. In the first eleven lines she lists various types of men that she likes — the list reads increasingly quickly as the poem goes on, suggesting that it might be almost limitless. The lack of punctuation — just commas used to list the types — also implies that this is a long list and that the types are not really very different or, at least, that the differences do not really matter very much.

The title and opening is deceptively simple: "men" and "I like". The "s" alliteration in the first line draws attention to the softness — almost innocence — of the first type. However, the wry little twist, "wash that someone else has done" hints that maybe she does not like men as much as she is suggesting initially. The texture of the outdoor type — "thin-skinned" and "crinkled" and the detail of the athlete who has to "stoop to hear" and the label "moneyed man" continues the light humour. Her position of superiority is firmly established with the "unironic" sort who understand literal meaning only and fail to laugh at jokes. She pokes fun at the pompous men with kids and cars who "own the earth" and those who don't know "born is hard". The final lines of this verse further establish the simplicity of all men in the poet's eyes: they "snatch" and catch clean the cricket ball. The onomatopoeia of "smack" and the alliteration of the "c" emphasises the simplicity.

The final couplet looks like a separate statement — and it is different in that it concerns the poet rather than her list of men. But it is also connected to the first eleven lines by the rhyme — "hand" and "land". There is a separation and a connection and this seems to describe the poet's relationship with men. She has established throughout the poem a distance between herself and them and her position of superiority — she is lightly laughing at them and she understands more than they do as the final metaphor suggests. She is the dark and mysterious continent round which these men "sail" (but never land?) because they understand very little. They are blinded by or confused in their journey and can only "peer" or look with suspicion or uncertainty at this unknown land.

However, the final word is puzzling: "laugh". This sentence seems to suggest that it is the men who laugh and yet the sense of the poem suggests that the poet in her superiority puts these men to sea and then she herself laughs as they are blinded in ignorance. This final ambiguity makes an interesting poem even a bit more puzzling. The half-rhyme throughout the poem with words that do not rhyme in a satisfying way prepares us for the ending. Are we laughing in fun or has the poet tricked us into accepting a note of bitterness in her description of the relationship with men?

THE WAY MY MOTHER SPEAKS

personal — (I) say her phrases to myself > *talking to herself*

in my head > *in her mind*

or under the shallows of my breath,

restful shapes moving. > *contradiction — oxymoron —* "restful" and "moving" at the same time

5   *The day and ever. The day and ever.*   *Italics indicate mother's speech. Also colloquial — a cliché*

           repetition

sound of words — long and slow — broad vowels — The train this ((slow) evening) *transferred epithet — can an evening be slow? the train is slow* *run-on lines*

(goes) (down) England

(brow) sing for the right sky,

(too) (blue) swapped for a (cool) grey. > *Scotland/England*

10   For miles I have been saying

repeated mother's words — colloquial — *What like is it*

the way I say things when I think.

Nothing is silent. Nothing is (not) silent. > *repetition — like sound of wheels of train on track, a contradiction — "silent" and "not silent"*

What like is it.

15   Only tonight > *importance of the night — one-off occasion*

I am happy and sad > *contradiction — both feelings at the same time*

like a child

who stood at the end of summer > *image — childhood like a season (summer)*

and dipped a net > *richness* — *but a pond is static — even stagnant at the end of summer*

full of life   *sexual* — in a (green), (erotic) (pond.) *The day and ever. The day and ever.* > *repeated like train wheels*

I am homesick, free, in love — *subtle contradiction*

with the way my mother speaks.

Main Techniques — *Consider how word choice, imagery and contradictions help to convey the poet's relationship with her mother.*

     Word choice   — *italics for mother's expressions*
                  oxymoron — transferred epithet
     Imagery   — *end of summer like end of childhood*
     Contradictions — *"restful shapes moving"*
                  cannot be silent — thoughts in her head
                  cannot be happy completely — sadness at leaving
                  cannot be free (homesick — tied to mother)

     Ideas   —   *Confused, contradictory ideas within the mind — importance of mother — impossibility of being free from her.*
                     Loss of childhood innocence with recognition of mother (and her words).
                     Journey by train a symbolic movement away from mother and home.

The Way My Mother Speaks explores the complex mother/child relationship. The persona (a young girl?) is travelling by train from Scotland to England. The poem is a stream-of-consciousness: the mind filled with thoughts of her mother and her mother's characteristic colloquial phrases in italics. She repeats these as if in time to the train's movements.

One of these phrases is a Scots dialectical phrase, "What like is it" or "What is it like". The repetition of this suggests that the persona would like to be telling her mother about the sort of things she is encountering on her journey. The other phrase is less well known, "The day and ever", literally, it is a contradiction: the day is twenty-four hours only; "ever" is eternity. Does it mean that it will be the same today as it is forever?

Other contradictions are present in the poem — in fact, to such an extent that contradiction seems an essential part of the themes. The phrase "restful shapes moving" is unusual. "Restful" and "moving" are opposites. Do the mother's phrases suggest peace and comfort; yet they keep repeating themselves in her head in a way that is perhaps unsettling? The phrase "slow evening" is unusual (a transferred epithet). The evening only seems slow because the train is slow, or, more likely, because time hangs heavily in the person's mind. Her thoughts make her journey long and tedious. The sound of these lines with the broad vowels (o and a) emphasises this tedium. It is impossible to read the first four lines of stanza two quickly: "The train this slow evening / goes down England / browsing . . .".

Another contradiction, "Nothing is silent. Nothing is not silent.", is even more puzzling. Is she suggesting that she would rid her mind of these thoughts and sayings — at least temporarily — but that she cannot? In the seeming silence, the mother's phrase, "What like is it" keeps repeating itself in her thoughts.

In the final stanza the paradoxical nature of the ideas, the conflicting feelings of the persona, intensify. When the poet says "only tonight", does she mean that the events of the evening are singular in raising these emotions and thoughts? Or does she mean "just" tonight for the first time, she has felt this way? She likens her conflicting emotions — "happy and sad" — to a time in childhood at the end of summer (season for fullness and play) when she fished from or "dipped a net" in a pond. The words "green" and "erotic" suggest the richness of life and the potential for creation in the still water. But a pond is self-contained, static and possibly even stagnant at the end of summer.

The last two lines focus on the tension of the contradiction: to be homesick and free at the same time. When the poet says she is "in love with the way my mother speaks", she is suggesting that she will never be "free" of her mother altogether; her mother's words will always be in her head (the day and ever). Physically or geographically, she might be "free"; emotionally and mentally, she will always be tied. The repetitive nature of the poem and the italicised phrases emphasise this parental dominance which, in fact, the persona considers in quite a fond and loving way. Perhaps this contradictory state is inevitable — the fate of the young.

CHAPTER 3

Appreciating the Poet's Tone

The poet can show through his tone his attitude to a subject or idea. In each of the poems in this section a poet is presenting his point of view or his ideas about a subject and the tone of voice he uses helps the reader to understand what he feels about the subject.

Stephen Crane is offering his view of war in *War is Kind* which is expressed in an unusual way. Try to determine exactly what Crane thinks about war.

John Fuller takes into consideration views on love — or more precisely — courtship in *Fairy Tale*. His poem has an unusual tone and it may not be immediately apparent what his real views are.

Kate Clanchy is commenting on the way young boys grow up in *Men from the Boys*. She does not, however, seem to be taking her subject entirely seriously.

Finally, Robert Crawford is giving some ideas about modern Scotland in *Alba Einstein*. Try to determine what he is commenting upon: Scotland, tourism, modern man generally?

Each of these poems is unusual and even striking in its "tone" or voice in which the poet expresses his or her opinions. Take notes on each poem, particularly noticing the unusual parts or puzzling phrases. Ask yourself whether or not you think the poet really means what he or she is saying in each case. Then go on to think about what this suggests about his point of view towards the subject in question. Remember that you cannot always take literally, or seriously, everything that a poet says; remember, too, that a serious point can be made with humour.

In trying to determine the tone of a poem, you as the reader are trying to establish a relationship with the poet in which you come as close as you can to understanding his point of view. Try to "hear" his tone through the words on the page.

WAR IS KIND

Do not weep, maiden, for war is kind.
Because your lover threw wild hands towards the sky
And the affrighted steed ran on alone,
Do not weep.
5   War is kind.

Hoarse, booming drums of the regiment,
Little souls who thirst for fight,
These men were born to drill and die,
The unexplained glory flies above them,
10   Great is the battle god, great, and his kingdom
A field where a thousand corpses lie.

Do not weep, babe, for war is kind.
Because your father tumbled in the yellow trenches,
Raged at his breast, gulped and died,
15   Do not weep.
War is kind.

Swift blazing flag of the regiment,
Eagle with crest of red and gold,
These men were born to drill and die.
20   Point for them the virtue of slaughter,
Make plain to them the excellence of killing
And a field where a thousand corpses lie.

Mother whose heart hung humble as a button
On the bright splendid shroud of your son,
25   Do not weep.
War is kind.

Stephen Crane

Understanding and Analysis

(a)   (i)   Explain to whom the poet is speaking and under what circumstances in the first stanza (lines 1–5).   **2**

     (ii)   By commenting on the choice of words in lines 1–5, say how the picture he presents is a contrast to "War is kind" (line 5).   **4**

(b)   The poet is adapting an ironic tone in this poem. Explain two ways in which he uses irony in stanza two (lines 6–11) to show his thinking.   **4**

(c)   Comment fully on the words in the third stanza (lines 12–16) which convey another unpleasant picture of war's effects.   **4**

(d)   (i)   Choose one of the symbols from stanza four (lines 17–22) and explain how it is used to suggest the glory of war.   **2**

     (ii)   Comment on the effectiveness of the tone in two of the following phrases:
        "born to drill and die" (line 19);
        "virtue of slaughter" (line 20);
        "excellence of killing" (line 21).   **4**

Evaluation

(e)   (i)   The last stanza (lines 23–26) presents the picture of a third person who suffers from war-time loss. Focusing on this image particularly as the final development of the poet's ideas, comment fully on how effective you find this image in conveying the poet's feelings about war.

     (ii)   You should then consider any of the relevant poetic techniques such as form, rhyme, rhythm, tone, word choice, imagery and symbols which you found helpful in understanding the poet's thoughts about war throughout the poem.   **10**

(30)

FAIRY TALE

Blushing, she fled: no one was on her side.
She could not bear the whistle and the slap,
The fustian* prospect of a farmer's lap.
Her father moped. Her sisters swore. She cried,
5   Dreamed of the Prince, neglected all her tasks
And now had run away, but not for long:
The wood was frightful as a wig, as wrong
As her own hearth. Soon she returned, through masks
Of mist. Her heart jumped at the stir that took
10   Her eye: the royal hounds sagged in the porch,
Their tongues like shoehorns. Someone waved a torch.
Hardly believing, breathless, she ran to look
But worse than all the sniggers of the wood,
The waiting Prince was ugly, pale and good.

John Fuller

* fustian —   This word has two very different meanings, both in keeping with this poem:
1. a kind of coarse, black twilled cotton cloth;
2. an inflated style of writing; a swelling above the dignity of the thoughts of the subject.

Understanding and Analysis

(a) Explain why, acording to lines 1–3, she might have run away embarrassed, "Blushing, she fled." 2

(b) A number of words in the first eight lines suggest which "Fairy Tale" might be the basis of this poem. Examine the implications of three of the following:

    (i)   "dreamed of the Prince" (line 5);
    (ii)   "neglected all her tasks" (line 5);
    (iii)   "her own hearth" (line 8);
    (iv)   "through masks" (line 8).   6

(c) How effective do you find the sentences of line 4 in terms of the narrative and as a poetic technique? 4

(d) Examine two unusual images and suggest any ways you can think of in which these odd comparisons might be said to be appropriate:

    (i)   "The wood was frightful as a wig" (line 7);
    (ii)   "Their tongues like shoehorns" (line 11).   4

(e) "Her heart jumped at the stir . . ." (line 9)

How does the poet make this an important moment in this poem? You might wish to consider word choice, enjambement, rhyme, poetic form or sentence structure in forming your judgement. 4

Evaluation

(f)   (i)   Consider particularly the twist in the final couplet of this poem. Explain why these lines are surprising.

       (ii)   To what extent do you find the ideas and presentation of these ideas humorous or light-hearted? Explain the ideas and techniques fully in your answer.   10

(30)

MEN FROM THE BOYS

Imagine this man as a lonely boy:
at the biscuit-smelling, sour milk stage,
shirt misbuttoned, strangled tie,
pockets stocked with fists and secrets.

5   The inky boy in the front row desk
who writes his name, address, adds
England, Earth, the Universe, concocts
a six month scheme for their general good;

gets dressed in robes to bury voles,
10   makes the cat a home that goes unused
or tries to help the birds with nests;
gives over spring to crushing flies

to keep a fledgling half alive; and spends
dank winter afternoons spinning
15   treacle over spoons or making tapes
of private jokes with laughter

added later. This boy writes runes
in milk on library books, and *Out*,
Forbidden on his door. You know
20   that if you grab him now

you'll hold a bag of kicking bones.
He wants no comfort, mother, home.
He'll work the whole thing out alone.

Kate Clanchy

Understanding and Analysis

(a)   (i)   Explain how the first stanza sets out the intention and the tone of the poem. You should pay particular attention to the words "Imagine" and "lonely boy".   **2**

       (ii)   Comment on how the details of the first verse convey the unsatisfactory condition of a very young boy.   **4**

       (iii)   What is unusual about the contents of the boy's pockets in line 4?   **2**

(b)   (i)   What does the phrase

> ". . . adds
> England, Earth, the Universe" (lines 6 and 7)

suggest to you about the boy?   **2**

       (ii)   Comment fully on the way in which other seemingly insignificant details actually convey a great deal about the boy in verses 2–5 (lines 5–19).   **6**

(c)

> ". . . You know
> that if you grab him now
>
> you'll hold a bag of kicking bones."   (lines 19–21)

These lines seem central to the ideas of the poem. Explain what they mean to you, perhaps concentrating particularly on the connotations of "grab" and "bag of kicking bones".   **4**

Evaluation

(d)   (i)   The final lines and the titles of poems are often significant to the meaning, sometimes because they are ambiguous. To what extent is this statement true of this poem?

       (ii)   You should explain fully what ideas emerge throughout the poem by referring closely to language features like word choice, imagery, run-on sentences, point of view, the title.   **10**

   (30)

ALBA EINSTEIN*

When proof of Einstein's Glaswegian birth
First hit the media everything else was dropped:
Logie Baird, Dundee painters, David Hume — all
Got the big E. Physics documentaries
5   Became peak-viewing; Scots publishers hurled awa
MacDiarmid like an overbaked potato, and swooped
On the memorabilia: *Einstein Used My Fruitshop*,
Einstein in Old Postcards, Einstein's Bearsden Relatives.
Hot on their heels came the A. E. Fun Park,
10   Quantum Court, Glen Einstein Highland Malt.
Glasgow was booming. Scotland rose to its feet
At Albert Suppers where The Toast to the General Theory
Was given by footballers, panto-dames, or restaurateurs.
In the U.S. an ageing lab-technician recorded
15   How the Great Man when excited showed a telltale glottal
           stop.
He'd loved fiddlers' rallies. His favourite sport was curling.
Thanks to this, Scottish business expanded
Endlessly. His head grew toby-jug-shaped,
20   Ideal for keyrings. He'd always worn brogues.
Ate bannocks in exile. As a wee boy he'd read *The Beano*.
His name brought new energy: our culture was solidly based
On pride in our hero, The Universal Scot.

Robert Crawford

* Albert Einstein was a famous scientist — a physicist — who is not Scottish.

Understanding and Analysis

(a) Show how two of the following phrases set the tone at the beginning of the poem:

    (i)   "hit the media" (line 2);

    (ii)   "Got the big E" (line 4);

    (iii) "Physics documentaries
          became peak viewing" (lines 4 and 5).   **4**

(b) Explain fully how the poet conveys his attitudes towards the reading public in the lines:

                  "Scots publishers hurled awa
          MacDiarmid like an overbaked potato."   (lines 5 and 6).   **4**

(c) Account for the italics in line 7 and the capital letters in line 12.   **2**

(d) Comment on the contribution which any two of the following make to the tone and meaning of the poem:

    (i)   A.E. Fun Park (line 9);

    (ii)   Quantum Court (line 10);

    (iii) Glen Einstein Highland Malt (line 10).   **4**

(e) Show two ways in which the sentence structure from line 14 to the end of the poem contributes to the idea that "Glasgow was booming" (line 11).   **4**

(f) "Brogues" (line 20), "bannocks" (line 21) and *The Beano* (line 21). How do two of these add to the humour of the poem?   **2**

Evaluation

(g)   (i)   The poet is perhaps poking fun at many aspects of modern Scottish life. To what extent do you think that the poet is making fun of modern Scots or to what extent is his point a more general one — a trait of human nature rather than of Scots particularly?

       (ii)   You should discuss the ideas conveyed throughout the poem giving consideration to such techniques as tone, word choice, structure, informality of language and/or title.   **10**

                                               (30)

WAR IS KIND — *odd*

command

addresses young woman

Do not weep (maiden,) for war is kind. > *untrue*

her lover is killed

Because your lover (threw) (wild) hands towards the sky

And the (affrighted) steed ran on alone,   *violent actions — fear? pain?*

Do not weep.   *picture of horror — frightened, riderless horse*

repetition

5   War is kind.

sound — personification of drums

Hoarse, (booming) drums of the regiment,   *yearning for war*

critical   (Little) souls who (thirst) for fight,

born to die —   These men were (born) to drill and (die,)   *alliteration draws attention to die*

oxymoron

patriotism   The (unexplained glory) flies above them,   *flag*

inexplicable

10   Great is the battle god, great, and his kingdom   *irony of glory in face of death*

A field where a thousand corpses lie. > *anti-climax — horror*

irony of being born to die

repetition emphasises irony

addresses baby

parallel structure to first stanza

Do not weep, (babe,) for war is kind.   *odd colour — sick*

Because your father (tumbled) in the (yellow) trenches,

anger at war or pain of dying   (Raged) at his (breast,) (gulped) and died,   *makes it sound softer — accidental*

15   Do not weep.   *vulnerable*   *human detail — unpleasant — suggests discomfort*

War is kind.

strong adjectives powerful glorious

(Swift) (blazing) flag of the regiment,   *the glory of war*

symbol of power/strength   (Eagle) with crest of (red) and (gold,) > *heraldic colours*

These men were (born) to drill and (die). *repetition of this odd idea — ironic*

20   Point for them the virtue of slaughter,

Make plain to them the excellence of killing   > *ironic — can there be virtue in killing? oxymoronic?*

And a field where a thousand corpses lie.

repetition

any mother — life-giving force — unnatural for mother to bury son

addresses mother changes form does not tell her not to weep

(Mother) whose heart hung humble as a button > *alliteration draws attention to odd image — heart hanging like a button*

On the (bright) (splendid) shroud of your son,   *oxymoron*

25   Do not weep.

War is kind.   *strange adjectives to use with shroud — garment of death should be uniform — buttons inappropriate on shroud*

Main Techniques — *Consider how the poet uses unusual contrasts and the structure of the poem to express a bitterness about the cruelty of war.*

Contrasts / Oxymorons / Juxtaposition — opposites are put together to show the irony

Structure — Repetition — three addresses to victims of war.

Tone — of irony — means the opposite of what it says

Ideas — The unexpected harshness of war when glory is expected.

In this short poem, *War Is Kind*, three poignant pictures of victims who suffer from the losses of war are presented. Perhaps the most moving picture is that of the final victim, a mother. However, it is the first two pictures which prepare us for the full significance and climatic nature of the third.

The first victim is a young girl who has lost her lover. The horror of her lover losing his life is shockingly conveyed with words like "threw" and "wild". He collapses to the ground in pain as he reaches "toward the sky". The further detail of the frightened horse galloping on riderless consolidates the horror. When the poet instructs the young girl, "Do not weep. War is kind," we know he is being ironic.

The usual signs of war's glory begin the second stanza: "booming drums", marching men and flying flags. However, the poet/persona is bitter when he calls men who do not think about the sacrifice of life in war "little souls" and says they "thirst" for a fight. The alliteration of "drill and die" draws attention to that phrase as if the two go together and ironic comment is even sharper in the idea of born to die. The word "unexplained" makes a critical comment on the supposed glory of the patriotic symbol of the flag. The final juxtaposition of the god of war with "great" — the word repeated twice — and his realm, a field of dead or dying corpses, is a central irony in the poem. The kingdom of war is inhabited only by the dead.

The poet tells the second victim, a baby, about the death of his father. Words like "tumbled" and "gulped" show the vulnerability of the soldier at his death. "Raged at his breast" could mean anger at the pain and grief of foreseeing his death or anger at having to fight at all — at the leaders who send men to slaughter. The "chorus" which follows uses the symbol of the flag by describing it with glowing words — "swift" and "blazing". The eagle is a symbol of power and might and "red and gold" are heraldic colours of war. The tone is even more ironic and bitter in "virtue of slaughter" and "excellence of killing" — another image of a field of corpses, the end result of supposed "virtue" or "excellence" which demands lives.

The final and, for me, most moving victim is a mother. The alliteration of the "h" draws attention to the picture and in likening the mother's heart to a button, not only the humility, but also the homeliness of the image is implied. A mother lovingly sews the buttons on her son's shirts — or uniforms. In this case the button is only needed for the shroud for a son who has died in war. The inappropriateness of a button on a shroud is highlighted by "bright" and "splendid", hardly words one would use to describe a garment of death.

The poet is most bitter in his depiction of this victim. Therefore, it is appropriate that he does not follow this image with a chorus because the image of the mother is like a climax to the images of war's "kindness". The poem ends with this shocking and moving result of war. Mother, a symbol of life and creation, sees her son to the grave in an unnatural way because men fight. The irony of "war is kind" in the final line and in the title is most convincing.

FAIRY TALE — *Cinderella — happily ever after?*

Annotations (left margin):
- Embarrassed < Blushing
- rough, coarse material / suggested courtship by a farmer (fustian)
- family reactions
- 5 Prince Charming
- odd image (wigs worn in days of Cinderella)
- cinders
- emotive dramatic
- 10 describes hounds
- good image to describe tongues but also suggests Cinderella tale

Poem:

(Embarrassed<) **Blushing,** she fled: no one was on her side. *a* > isolated

She could not bear the whistle and the slap, *b* — coarse gestures of attention that cause embarrassment

The (fustian) prospect of a farmer's lap. *b*

(family reactions<) Her father moped. Her sisters swore. She cried, *a* — short sharp sentences emphasise action and drama

Dreamed of the (Prince), neglected all her tasks *c* > sounds like Cinderella working

And now had run away, but not for long: *d* — a wig is a disguise

The wood was (frightful as a (wig)), (as wrong *d* — odd image

As her own (hearth).) Soon she returned, through (masks) *c* — masks at a costume ball

Of mist. Her (heart jumped) at the stir that took *e* — alliteration / enjambement emphasise confusion — mistaken identity

Her eye (:) the royal hounds (sagged) in the porch, *f*

Their tongues (like shoehorns.) Someone waved a torch. *f*

Hardly believing, breathless, she ran to look *e* > build-up — climax

But worse than all the (sniggers) of the wood, *g* > coarse observers

The waiting Prince was ugly, pale and good. *g* — odd combination of adjectives. Is Prince a disappointment? Tall, dark, handsome is expected. Good is odd final word.

surprise ending turns "happily ever after" on its head

Main Techniques — Consider how the poet uses imagery and the structure of the poem to establish a tone which is light-hearted and mocking.

Structure — sonnet — 14 lines — quatrains rhyme plus couplet. Traditional form for traditional fairy tale

Tone — mocks fairy tale idea and happy endings

Imagery — unusual pictures are original and humorous

Ideas — Uses tradition — form and fairy tale — to mock the usual idea of courtship in a humorous way. Suggests the "dark wood" of relationships with humour.

Fairy Tale is a parody of Cinderella. The sisters (ugly or merely coarse?), the tasks, the hearth, the shoehorns, and finally the Prince give it away. It is making light of the business of finding a husband. In the first eight lines of this modern sonnet, the young girl runs embarrassed alone from the idea of marrying a crude, coarse type suggested by "whistle", "slap" and "farmer's lap" as she longed for a Prince. The word "fustian" with its two very different meanings suggests the coarseness of this lap and the inflated ideas that the young girl might have and also possibly warns the reader not to take this subject too seriously. Was this an arranged marriage that she rejected to the upset of her sullen father and her angered sisters? The short sentences of line 4 suggest the dramatic and varying reactions of the family.

The flight is to the wood. The unusual image draws attention to the superficiality of the courting ritual. The wood is "frightful as a wig" — some of these artificial creations that resemble hair are awesome because they change a person's natural appearance. When she returns home it is through "masks of mist". This phrase reinforces the idea of superficiality, of hiding behind a false front.

A change is sudden when in a new sentence we are told "her heart jumped", for as she returns home she sees the royal hounds with their tongues "like shoehorns" reminding us of Cinderella and suggesting that the Prince is looking for a match. The drama increases as the torch waves and her reaction is "hardly believing" and "breathless".

However, the final couplet is an anticlimax. Now that she has faced the evils of the wood, the Prince is, disappointingly, not only ugly and pale, but also good. The poet seems to be poking fun at the artificial values of fairy tales: tall-dark-and-handsome and happily-ever-after. The ambiguity of the word "fustian" early in the poem hints that we are to keep this subject matter in perspective. Nevertheless, the poet's use of the sonnet with the tight rhyme scheme (*a b b a, c d d c, e f f e* in the first twelve lines) draws attention to the mocking tone. The conclusive couplet (*g g*), in a traditional form of poetry and the idea of a traditional fairy tale are used to draw attention with a light and humorous tone to the superficial values of matrimony and courtship.

MEN FROM THE BOYS

Two meanings to title
Separate the men from the boys
Men emerge from boys

command　　　*sympathetic*

Imagine this man as a *lonely* boy: ＞ *reflect on origins of this boy*

young
not very pleasant

at the *biscuit-smelling, sour milk* stage,

negative connotations, unpleasant

shirt *misbuttoned, strangled* tie,

pockets stocked with *fists* and *secrets.*

odd combination — *"secrets" suggests*
boyish world of
delights rather than
contents of pockets

youthful — but disorganised / uncomfortable

messy

5　The *inky* boy in the front row desk

who writes his name, address, adds

England, Earth, the Universe, *concocts*

shows immaturity
— *suggests oddness*

a six month *scheme* for their general good; ＞ *immaturity again /*
control the world

childish plans

gets *dressed* in robes to bury voles, —— *childish action*

10　makes the cat a home that goes unused ＞ *impractical*

or *tries to help* the birds with nests; ＞ *unrealistic*

youthful idealism

gives over spring to crushing flies ＞ *cruel — but to a purpose — feeding*
a young bird

to keep a fledgling half alive; and spends ＞ *kind*

dank winter afternoons spinning

15　treacle over spoons or making tapes ——— *variety of activities*

of private jokes with laughter

run-on
lines draw
attention to this
variety
— adds humour

(added later.) This boy writes runes *sound*

in milk on library books, and *Out,* —— *asserting authority*

Forbidden on his door. *You* know

change in point of view — to reader

20　that if you *grab* him now

suffocating ——— *connotations of force*

you'll hold a *bag* of (kicking bones.) — *no flesh — physically and*
emotionally incomplete

independence — He wants no comfort, mother, home. —
abstracts

He'll work the whole *thing* out *alone.*

vague　　　*isolation*

Main Techniques — *Consider all the devices the poet uses — words, imagery, title to create exaggerated effects and humour.*

Words — *connotations that convey isolation, efforts at independence*

Images — *poem starts with the word "Imagine"*
collection of details and images about the "lonely boy"

Title — *two meanings that lead into ideas*

Last line — *emphasis on ideas of isolation and independence*

Tone — *humorous, exaggerated, all-knowing — giving "advice" to reader.*

Ideas — *Rites of passage. Natural progression of youth from childhood to independence.*

In *Men from the Boys,* the poet orders us to try to imagine "this man" as a "lonely boy", but the man could, in fact, be anyone. The first stage of such imagining depicts a boy at a very young age — smelling of biscuits and sour milk — not altogether pleasant. The carefully selected details suggest the extreme youthfulness and even discomfort of the individual with his shirt wrongly buttoned and the tie sitting uncomfortably round his neck. The word "stocked" suggests a richness of precious objects — a readiness to burst into living.

The details which follow suggest a slightly older, but still unsettled, youth, who immaturely includes, "England, Earth, the Universe" to his address and overall identification. His schemes and plans show childish enthusiasm from ceremonially burying wild animals to constructing carefully for a cat a home that is never used. The care and attention to nature and wildlife is conveyed in the details of attempting to feed futilely a half-dead bird and idealistically trying to help birds build nests. Then carefully selected details awaken common memories of similar weekend projects of youthful days. The sign "Out, Forbidden" on the door indicates the desire for privacy and hints at what is to come in the last verse of the poem.

The poet takes a step back from his close observation of the boy in the fifth verse with his address to the reader, "You know", and reminds us that she is giving us a little instruction about life. The use of the word "grab" suggests that if you want to have or to hold this boy now, you would have to use force and come upon him unaware. Even if you were successful in catching him physically, the poet warns ominously that you would have gathered very little — "a bag of kicking bones". This phrase suggests to us that the boy would have to be captured and held in an almost suffocating way (bag) to arrest his movement and development and also that the prize would be worthless. Bones only — no flesh — for this youth is developing — physically, emotionally, intellectually, morally — in every sense.

The final lines remind us that this is a growing individual. Everyone goes through the same process and this sort of rite of passage must be endured "alone" — a harkening back to our imagining a "lonely boy" in verse one. What the boy is working out is vague — "the whole thing" — life in general, but the comforts of childhood must be abandoned at this stage.

The title could be ambiguous. It literally suggests that men come from such boys, but it also suggests to me the phrase "separating the men from the boys". Could the poet be implying that grabbing a boy at such a stage of growth and passage and suffocating or arresting his development might leave you with "bones" — fleshless and unfeeling — the eternal adolescent? And the final question: why not women from girls?

Old name for Scotland — play on name "Albert"

(ALBA) EINSTEIN

slang
humorous
light-hearted

When proof of <u>Einstein's Glaswegian birth</u> > *not true*

First (hit the media) everything else was dropped:

Logie Baird, Dundee painters, David Hume — all > *genuinely famous Scots*

(Got the big E.) Physics documentaries > *odd*

5 *humorous image* (Became peak-viewing) ; Scots publishers <u>hurled awa</u> > *Scots dialect*

MacDiarmid (like an overbaked potato,) and (swooped) —— *like predators*

On the memorabilia: *Einstein Used My Friendship,* 〉 *mocking — italics*
suggest importance

Einstein in Old Postcards, Einstein's Bearsden Relatives. *almost like titles*

slang — (Hot on their heels) came the <u>A.E. Fun Park</u>, > *pokes fun at commercialisation*

typical name of malt whisky

10 *sound* Quantum <u>C</u>ourt, (Glen) Einstein Highland Malt.
sentence is a —
climax (Glasgow was booming.) <u>Scotland rose to its feet</u> — *personification of nation*

mock of At <u>A</u>lbert <u>S</u>uppers where <u>T</u>he <u>T</u>oast to the <u>G</u>eneral <u>T</u>heory — *capital letters*
Burns Suppers *suggest it is a*

Was given by footballers, panto-dames, or restaurateurs. *tradition*

In the U.S. an ageing lab-technician recorded *"enjambement emphasises*
endlessly"

15 How the Great Man when excited showed a telltale <u>glottal</u>

    stop. > *typically Scottish*

He'd loved <u>fiddlers' rallies</u>. His favourite sport was <u>curling</u>.

Thanks to this, Scottish business expanded *enjambement emphasises "endlessly"*

Endlessly. (His head grew toby-jug-shaped, *Items for tourists*

20 Ideal for keyrings.) He'd always worn <u>b</u>rogues. – *Scottish kilt shoes*

Ate (bannocks) in exile. As a (wee) boy he'd read *The <u>B</u>eano*. — *typically Scottish*

Scottish food His name brought new (energy) our culture was solidly based

pun? On pride in our hero, The Uni<u>v</u>ersal Scot. > *capital letters*
theories of *draw attention*
energy ∨ *Scots* *to exaggeration*
tone *— a concept*

Main Techniques — *Consider how the poet uses exaggerated images and words and colloquial language to mock*
commercialisation and over-zealous patriotism.
Register — *slang / colloquial — makes poem light-hearted.*
Images — *word choice — outrageous and exaggerated in choice of details.*
Tone — *parody — mocks efforts to commercialise tourist attraction; also mocks overly-patriotic attitudes*

Ideas — *Humorous criticism of over-enthusiastic patriotism.*
Critical of commercialisation.

Alba Einstein is a light-hearted poem — even in the title, which changes the great scientist's name. The poet is drawing attention to and poking fun at the modern inclination to claim all the best for one's own nation; he becomes even more critical and sharply satirical when he shows that there is money to be made in laying claim to the greats. The colloquial language (even slang at points) is tongue-in-cheek from the beginning of the poem and media-driven: "first hit the media" and "got the big E" for the other famous Scots (genuine Scots unlike Einstein). There is humour in the unlikelihood of Physics documentaries becoming "peak-viewing" — a comment on man's passing fancies and ability to watch even what he does not like if there might be a buck to be made.

The poet uses the Scots language effectively when he says MacDiarmid is "hurled awa" and presumably all written efforts concentrate on Alba Einstein. The reading public is just as fickle as the viewing public in their rapidly changing tastes. The italicised words show the possibilities for capitalising on Einstein's name in tourist centres and gift shops. The colloquial phrase "hot on their heels" continues to make light of the market for tourists — Alba Einstein Fun Parks, restaurants or hotels named after his theories and even Scottish malt being marketed with the Einstein label. The italics suggest the importance of souvenirs — almost like titles.

The second half of the poem uses sentence structure effectively to bombard the reader with a list of humorous and idiosyncratic possibilities. The poet is making fun of the commercialisation of other heroes like R. Burns. The well-known Scottish "glottal stop" is brought in for proof of authenticity. Then the list of Einstein's likes becomes endless — fiddlers' rallies, curling and *The Beano*. Markets for trinkets, toby jugs and key rings, and traditional dress and food — brogues and bannocks — are all money-making possibilities.

Crawford is criticising much about modern life in a light-hearted way. We find because of his humorous tone that by the end of the poem we have accepted criticism of: the parochial nature of patriotic pride; the modern tendency to make money out of anything in the twentieth century tourist trade; and finally, and perhaps most significantly, the loss of any really distinctive features of our national identity that make Scots different from Americans.

CHAPTER 4

Understanding Ideas through the Structure of a Poem

Many poems can be understood better if the reader can see how the poet's mind was working when he structured his poem. In this chapter, the four poems offered are structured in a way that might help you to see the ideas better.

William B. Yeats uses rhyme to structure his poem *An Irish Airman Foresees His Death*. When you take notes on the poem, notice how the rhyme divides it into sections. Identify the main idea of each section. How does each "rhyming section" relate to the other sections?

Seamus Heaney clearly divides his poem *At the Wellhead* into two main sections. Again, ask yourself what the difference is. Perhaps, more significantly, what are the similarities between the two sections?

In *Design*, Robert Frost uses the form of a sonnet to express his ideas. Use the rhyme scheme to identify the two parts of the sonnet and try to determine the different angle the poet is taking in each section. Can you arrive at any conclusions about the ideas of the poem from your analysis of this form?

In another sonnet, one by Shakespeare, the rhyme scheme suggests that you should divide the poem into three quatrains and a couplet. Ask yourself why these divisions? What similarities can you see between each of the quatrains? Notice the repetition in terms of structure as well as in terms of ideas. Can you see any differences, that is, any development or change from one quatrain to the next and does this lead you into understanding the ideas better?

A comparison of your jottings with the ones on the given poem should help you to identify changes or similarities that you might not have noticed in each case.

AN IRISH AIRMAN FORESEES HIS DEATH

I know that I shall meet my fate
Somewhere among the clouds above;
Those that I fight I do not hate,
Those that I guard I do not love;
5 My country is Kiltartan Cross,
My countrymen Kiltartan's poor,
No likely end could bring them loss
Or leave them happier than before
Nor law, nor duty bade me fight,
10 Nor public men, nor cheering crowds,
A lonely impulse of delight
Drove to this tumult in the clouds;
I balanced all, brought all to mind,
The years to come seemed waste of breath,
15 A waste of breath the years behind
In balance with this life, this death.

W.B. Yeats

Understanding and Analysis

(a) From the title and the first two lines of the poem, explain who the speaker is and what you think the poem will be about. **2**

(b) (i) The poet uses parallel structure (two sentences following the same form) in lines 3 and 4. How does this structure help to balance the ideas expressed in these lines? **4**

  (ii) Find in the poem another example of parallel structure, and explain how this technique helps you to understand the meaning of the lines in which it is used. **4**

(c) (i) Say in your own words what reasons airmen might have for enlisting according to lines 9 and 10. **4**

  (ii) Go on to explain how word choice in line 11 helps you to understand more fully this airman's reason for enlisting. **2**

(d) How do the final four lines help you to understand the airman's attitude towards his fate? **2**

(e) What does the title suggest to you about the airman's attitude? **2**

Evaluation

(f) Yeats is writing about war and death. Explain in detail how this subject is treated in this particular poem and what ideas the poet has suggested to you.

  You might consider how the rhyme scheme divides the poem into sections and how these sections are related. You might also wish to consider his treatment of his subject through sentence structures, word choice, tone and even the title itself. **10**

(30)

AT THE WELLHEAD

Your songs, when you sing them with your two eyes
    closed
As you always do, are like a local road
We've known every turn of in the past —
5   That midge-veiled, high-hedged side-road where you
    stood
Looking and listening until a car
Would come and go and leave you lonelier
Than you had been to begin with. So, sing on,
10   Dear shut-eyed one, dear fat-voiced veteran,

Sing yourself to where the singing comes from,
Ardent and cut off like our blind neighbour
Who played the piano all day in her bedroom.
Her notes came out to us like hoisted water
15   Ravelling off a bucket at the wellhead
Where next thing we'd be listening, hushed and
    awkward.

*

That blind-from-birth, sweet-voiced, withdrawn
    musician
20   Was like a silver vein in heavy clay.
Night water glittering in the light of day.
But also just our neighbour, Rosie Keenan.
She touched our cheeks. She let us touch her braille
In book like books wallpapers patterns came in.
25   Her hands were active and her eyes were full
Of open darkness and a watery shine.

She knew us by our voices. She'd say she 'saw'
Whoever or whatever. Being with her
Was intimate and helpful, like a cure
30   You didn't notice happening. When I read
A poem with Keenan's well in it, she said,
'I can see the sky at the bottom of it now.'

Seamus Heaney

Understanding and Analysis

(a) (i)   In the first section of the poem, the poet is picturing a singer whose eyes are closed. He likens the songs to a road. In what way does he make this unusual comparison appropriate in lines 3 and 4? **2**

     (ii) How effective is the word choice and sound of line 5 in helping you to picture aspects of the road? **4**

(b) (i)   What do you think the poet means by line 11:

           "Sing yourself to where the singing comes from"?

           Do the words "shut-eyed" (line 10) and "cut-off" (line 12) help in your understanding? **2**

     (ii) Two musicians are compared. The second, Rosie Keenan, the poet's neighbour, has been "blind-from-birth" unlike the "shut-eyed one". What similarity between the two is apparent? **2**

(c) He likens Rosie's piano playing to "hoisted water ravelling off a bucket at the wellhead" (lines 14 and 15). In what ways does this comparison seem appropriate? **4**

(d) Suggest why the listeners might feel "awkward" (line 17). How does the poet put emphasis on this idea? **2**

(e) The poet continues in the second section of this poem to explore the ideas introduced in the first section:

     (i)   isolation of the singer or the artist;
     (ii) the sources of music or creativity.

     How do any two examples of word choice, imagery or contrast used in lines 11–17 help you to understand one of these ideas better? **4**

Evaluation

(f) (i)   From line 18 to the end of the poem, Heaney is exploring the idea of "seeing" or understanding through the sense of sound and touch as well as through the sense of sight. In lines 18–26, comment on two of the images of "seeing" which Heaney uses.

     (ii) What ideas does Heaney convey to you about the nature of "seeing", particularly in the final line with Rosie Keenan's words? **10**

(30)

DESIGN

I found a dimpled spider, fat and white
On a white heal-all, holding up a moth
Like a white piece of rigid satin cloth —
Assorted characters of death and blight
5   Mixed ready to begin the morning right,
Like ingredients of a witches' broth —
A snow-drop spider, a flower like a froth,
And dead wings carried like a paper kite.

What had that flower to do with being white,
10   The wayside blue and innocent heal-all?
What brought the kindred spider to that height,
Then steered the white moth thither in the night?
What but design of darkness to appall? —
If design govern in a thing as small.

Robert Frost

Understanding and Analysis

(a) (i) In what way does the choice of words to describe the spider in line 1 seem inappropriate or surprising?   **3**

(ii) Explain how the poet suggests fragility and beauty in any two of the following images:

"a moth / like a white piece of satin cloth" (lines 2 and 3);
"a flower like a froth" (line 7);
"dead wings carried like a paper kite." (line 8).   **6**

(b) Trace the way in which light and darkness or opposites are connected in the first eight lines of this poem.   **4**

(c) What ideas does the poet convey to you through his use of sentence structure and repetition in the sestet (lines 9–14)?   **6**

(d) Explain how the rhyme scheme reinforces the idea in the title.   **1**

Evaluation

(e) (i) The first eight lines of this sonnet set out a puzzle or a problem. Considering your understanding of word choice, imagery, and contrast, state in your own words what the problem seems to be.

(ii) Then go on to consider how the ideas of the sestet relate to this problem.

You might wish to consider the sense — and especially the tone — of the last two lines in particular.   **10**

(30)

SONNET 73

That time of year thou mayst in me behold
When yellow leaves, or none, or few, do hang
Upon those boughs which shake against the cold,
Bare ruined choirs, where late the sweet birds sang.

5   In me thou see'st the twilight of such day
As after sunset fadeth in the west,
Which by and by black night doth take away,
Death's second self that seals up all in rest.
In me thou see'st the glowing of such fire

10   That on the ashes of his youth doth lie,
As the death bed whereon it must expire,
Consumed with that which it was nourished by.
    This thou perceivest, which makes thy love more strong
    To love that well which thou must leave ere long.

Shakespeare

Understanding and Analysis

(a)   The poet is likening his stage of life to autumn in the first four lines of the sonnet. Explain fully the image contained in lines 3 and 4 and how it suggests the change of seasons.   **4**

(b)   "Death's second self" (line 8) means sleep which has the appearance of death. Show how this image is consistent with the time of day and life being described in lines 5–8.   **4**

(c)   (i)   Explain what time is being described in line 9.   **1**

         (ii)   Choose two words from lines 9–12 and explain how each one has unpleasant or ominous suggestions.   **2**

(d)   Divide the poem into quatrains — three four-line sections.

         (i)   Explain the central concern of each section or quatrain.   **6**

         (ii)   Comment on any change or development that you can see from one section to the others.   **3**

Evaluation

(e)   (i)   Line 12 and the final two lines (a rhyming couplet) each contains a paradox or difficult puzzle. Say, in your own words, what you think the paradox is.

         (ii)   Go on to explain how the development of the poem in structure and in the central images of time help you to understand the ideas of the poem that lead to this concluding paradox.   **10**

     (30)

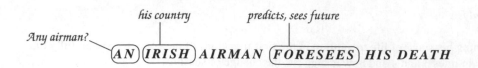

Any airman? — AN IRISH AIRMAN FORESEES HIS DEATH

his country (IRISH) — his country
predicts, sees future (FORESEES) — predicts, sees future

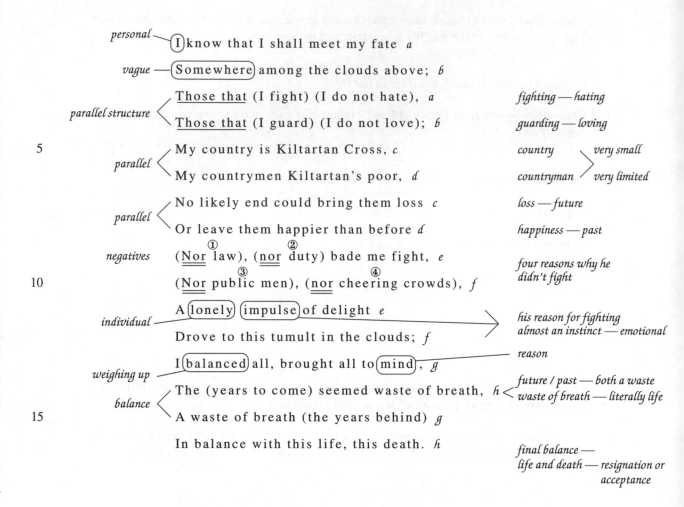

personal — I know that I shall meet my fate a

vague — Somewhere among the clouds above; b

parallel structure {
Those that (I fight) (I do not hate), a — fighting — hating
Those that (I guard) (I do not love); b — guarding — loving
}

5

parallel {
My country is Kiltartan Cross, c — country — very small
My countrymen Kiltartan's poor, d — countryman — very limited
}

parallel {
No likely end could bring them loss c — loss — future
Or leave them happier than before d — happiness — past
}

negatives — (Nor① law), (nor② duty) bade me fight, e
10
(Nor③ public men), (nor④ cheering crowds), f — four reasons why he didn't fight

individual — A lonely impulse of delight e
Drove to this tumult in the clouds; f — his reason for fighting almost an instinct — emotional

weighing up — I balanced all, brought all to mind, g — reason

balance {
The (years to come) seemed waste of breath, h — future / past — both a waste
waste of breath — literally life
A waste of breath (the years behind) g
}
15

In balance with this life, this death. h — final balance — life and death — resignation or acceptance

---

Main Techniques — Ask yourself why this poem is so carefully balanced and structured in sentences, rhyme and rhythm.

Parallel sentence structure showing balance: hating/loving, past/future, life/death and reasons/impulse
Regularity of rhythm and rhyme → the predictable nature or foreseeing the future
Tone — personal reflection, resigned acceptance of fate.

Ideas — "Reason" for fighting is an "impulse of delight" — the individual or lonely aspect of the man is realised because he seems different in his understanding and yet he is everyman — an Irish airman.
Also his "country" is a very small area — not even a village but a crossroads.
An anti-war poem which dismisses usual patriotic reasons for enlisting.

The title of the poem, *An Irish Airman Foresees His Death*, suggests what it is about. The speaker is not a special airman and he does not even have a name, but he tells us that he is resigned to his fate which he foresees or predicts will be in battle "somewhere" in the clouds. The two similar sentences (parallel sentence structure) in lines three and four set the tone for the poem and his thoughts. He does not fight savagely because he loves those he is defending. He thinks on a more specific local level: his home is Kiltartan Cross, suggesting a mere crossroads, not even a village. His "countrymen" are his neighbours, poor like himself, and he does not deceive himself into thinking that his efforts are going to make them any better or worse off than they would have been anyway.

He also balances his reasons for flying against reasons that other soldiers and airmen might offer (using parallel structure again). The list of four negatives emphasises that he was not called to enlist by conscription, or by a sense of duty, or by the rhetoric of persuasive politicians, or even the promise of glory in marching off to war midst "cheering crowds". He weighs up his reason against these other possibilities: his was an "impulse", a feeling or a strong desire which he alone felt to thrill or "delight" in the flying above the clouds, even though it be in chaotic battle or tumult.

The rhyme scheme divides the poem into four sections with a simple pattern of *a b a b*. The rhyme invites us to consider the ideas in each of these sections: the first section indicates the speaker's resigned attitude to his fate; the second considers his loyalty to the very small area of the country which is his; the third gives his reason for enlisting balanced against the reasons that might be cited more commonly; and the final section invites us to put the speaker's thinking into a larger context of life and death, past and present.

The last four lines is the final weighing up in the poem. "Brought all to mind" can be taken literally here for he thinks about his reasons. The "waste of breath" can also be taken literally for life is balanced against death. The tone of the poem and poet/persona is one of resignation. Even the sound of the last line is balanced, "this life, this death". The emphasis falls on this final word of the poem and the final word of the title. Death makes life seem futile and unimportant: all the more so in war when the sacrifice is by the young and it seems an unnecessary waste. The anonymous airman reminds us that his fate is every man's although his circumstances make death premature and all the more futile.

AT THE WELLHEAD — *source of water — symbolic*

Your songs, when you sing them with your two eyes
    closed   > *picture singer with eyes closed*
As you always do, are like a local road > *image. Song like a familiar road —*
We've known every turn of in the past ⊖ *break*   *turns and twists but well known*

5   That <u>midge-veiled</u>, <u>high-hedged</u> <u>side-road</u> where you
    stood *hyphenated words emphasising difficulty in seeing — notice "d" sound*
<u>Looking</u> and <u>listening</u> until a car > *sight and sound*
Would come and go and leave you lonelier *isolation*
Than you had been to begin with. (So,) sing on, *result*

10 Dear (shut-eyed) one, dear <u>fat-voiced</u> (veteran,) *suggests age*
    alone *hyphenated*
Sing yourself to where the singing comes from, — *the soul? inside?*
Ardent and (cut off) (like our blind neighbour) *similarity of another person — both*
Who played the piano all day in her bedroom *isolated — both sing "shut-eyed"*
Her notes came out to us (like hoisted water) *image — song drawn up from well-*

spilling off <u>Ravelling off</u> a bucket at the wellhead *odd*
    sound — quiet
15 Where next thing we'd be listening, (hushed) and *listening to something private?*
continuously <u>awkward</u>. > *not really part of experience or song — on line by itself*

                         *

< *Two parts — two musicians*
That <u>blind-from-birth</u>, <u>sweet-voiced</u>, (withdrawn) *isolated*
    musician *hyphenated words again*
20 Was (like a silver vein in heavy clay.) > *simile — valuable streak in mass — light,*
metaphor of (Night water glittering in the light of day.) *shiny in dark soil*
light and But also just our neighbour, Rosie Keenan.
darkness She <u>touched</u> our cheeks. She let us <u>touch</u> her braille > *sense of touch*
childish < In books like books <u>wallpapers patterns</u> came in.
repetition
25 Her hands were active and (her eyes were full) > *simile of feeling and touch*
                        blind — but she could "see"
positive < Of (open darkness) and a (watery shine). *odd combination*
connotation
to darkness (She knew us by our voices.) She'd say she 'saw' *didn't really see —*
                           inverted commas
Whoever or whatever. Being with her *important statement — "heard" knowledge*
                          through sound
30 *closeness* <u>Was intimate</u> and helpful, (like a cure
You didn't notice happening.) When I read > *image of healing*
A poem with Keenan's well in it, she said,
('I can see the sky at the (bottom) of it now.') *key line.*
                   sky — reflected in bottom of well?
    "see" meaning understanding *depths — inside — cut off — in darkness*

Main techniques — *Ask yourself why the poem is divided into two and what the details in each half come to symbolise.*
Symbolism — *wellhead — inner depths — resources; water — purity/innocence; sky — goals/aims*
Structure — *two singers — similarities and differences; both sing without their eyes*
Senses — *importance of sight and touch*
Similes and metaphors — *"like hoisted water", "like a silver vein", "like books", "like a cure".*
Ideas — *Quiet, inner self, "open darkness" is our source of inspiration. We "see" with our souls.*

At the Wellhead, rich in sensual imagery and contrasts, explores the idea of "seeing" in the sense of knowing or understanding. Heaney uses comparisons which depend upon sound and touch as well as sight. The poem tells of two musicians, one who sings with her eyes closed, and a "blind neighbour", Rosie Keenan, who plays the piano.

The song of the shut-eyed singer is compared to a local road. The unusual comparison is appropriate as both are forms of connecting people. A "local" road is also familiar — "We've known every turn in the past" — like a familiar song often heard which meanders, turns, twists (as the first stanza of this poem does as it runs on from line to line). The difficulty in seeing is highlighted in the unusual hyphenated words: "midge-veiled" suggests hazy vision; "high-hedged" implies difficulty in getting a view; and "side-road" indicates a little-travelled, less familiar route. The occasional car shows the isolation. The poem extends this idea of isolation with words like "cut-off". The blind neighbour was also isolated in "her bedroom" playing the piano alone. The source of music becomes important for the singer is to "sing yourself to where the singing comes from". The notes on the piano are like "hoisted water" reminding us of the title *At the Wellhead.* The source is a depth, a darkness. The listener might feel "hushed" or awed and "awkward" realising that they are listening to the soul, music coming from a musician's inner self.

Rosie Keenan shows not only the source of music, but also the idea that "seeing" is more than just visual. The imagery is also more than visual: it is aural and tactile for this is how Rosie "sees". She is "silver vein in heavy clay". The contrast in this image can be explored fully: silver sparkles, is light, mercurial, difficult to touch and impossible to hold — and valuable; heavy clay is ordinary, weighty, solid, unmoving, sticky and unattractive. Rosie's eyes are "full of open darkness" which suggests both depth of understanding and the blindness of sight. The simple sentences emphasise the obvious way to understand: touching cheek, touching braille. The braille feels like embossed wallpaper patterns. She also understands by hearing — knowing people by their voices.

The end of the poem is touching in every sense. The word "intimate" suggests the nature of the relationship with Rosie. Knowing her was not a matter of recognition through sight, but involved an intimacy of touching, hearing and "seeing" into the inner self. Being with her was "like a cure".

The final lines suggest that the poet once read one of his poems to this neighbour, mentioning "Keenan's well". Her comment, the final line, is revealing: "I can see the sky at the bottom of it now". She understood it and — even more — she saw the reflection of the sky in its very depths and darkness. The sky suggests the heights, the goals. Instead of looking upwards for our inspiration, perhaps we should look inward to our lonely depths. In an age which depends on knowing by seeing with the eye, much is overlooked. Perhaps, like the "fat-voiced veteran", we should close our eyes and "see" in isolation using other senses, including intuition, the source of which is *At the Wellhead.*

DESIGN — *implies theme — overall plan*

sounds appealing — not the usual description of spider

wrong colour — usually black

personal

wild flower — usually blue

I found a (dimpled) spider, (fat) and (white)   a

On a white (heal-all,) holding up a moth   b

clean innocent

Like a (white) piece of (rigid satin cloth) —   b   *simile — texture/colour of moth*

cloth used in a coffin

Assorted characters of (death) and (blight)   a   *negative connotations*

5   Mixed ready to begin the (morning) right,   a   *new, fresh*

Like ingredients of a witches' broth —   b   *simile — mysterious ingredients*

supernatural — evil

melt
a flower beautiful — short-lived

A (snow-drop) spider, a flower like a (froth,)   b   *blow away*

And dead wings carried <u>like a paper kite</u>.   a   *all fragile — lack substance*

tear — fragile — a thing to play with

①
What had that flower to do with being white,   a

10   The wayside blue and innocent heal-all (?)   c

②
parallel structure   What brought the kindred spider to that height,   a

Then steered the white moth thither in the night (?)   a

③
3 questions   What but design of darkness to appall (?)   c

conditional expresses an uncertainty   (If) design govern in a thing as small.   c

contrasts between:
white / night
life / death
great / small

Main techniques — *Ask why the poet uses a sonnet form. Does it reflect at all on the ideas of the poem?*

    Structure — *sonnet — octave sets up three "ingredients"; sestet poses three questions about design tight rhyme scheme*

    Word choice — *unusual details and descriptions for each item fragility / vulnerability brought out for each*

    Punctuation — *questions explore overall plan or design (title).*

Ideas — *Asking if there is an overall plan or are we all on our own in a terrifying way.*
Predestination? or Chance?

Design is a sonnet with an octave which presents a problem and a sestet which presents a resolution or rather a series of questions resulting from the problem. Three "ingredients" of a witches' broth suggest a design of evil or the supernatural. The spider is likened to a snow drop, but it sounds attractive, unusual for a spider. It is described as "dimpled", "fat and white". The stark contrast between the idea of the spider and the innocence and purity is striking.

The second ingredient, the victim, a moth, is described as "rigid", a word giving the sense of stiffness in death while at the same time presenting a picture of a piece of satin cloth standing upright. The fragility of the moth is shown by comparison to a paper kite.

The final ingredient, the white heal-all, is described as "like a froth" which suggests its transcience: blooming momentarily and likely to blow away, like the paper kite.

The sestet in *Design* is effective with a series of three parallel questions asking how each of these unusual items came to be at this point at that particular moment "in the night". The simplicity of the pattern helps to keep in mind the idea that the poet is asking whether there is an overall design to creation.

The final two lines of the sonnet are striking. The darkness of night contrasts with the white of the spider, flower and moth. The conditional "if" in the final line and the last word "small" is also convincing in terms of ideas. If there is a design that brought these three small ingredients together, is there a design in the affairs of men? The question is asked clearly.

Each detail of *Design* is in keeping with the ideas. The techniques, particularly the sonnet form, the word choice, and the rhetorical questions, are used to further the reflection on man's fate and the possibility of an overall scheme or design in our affairs.

SONNET 73

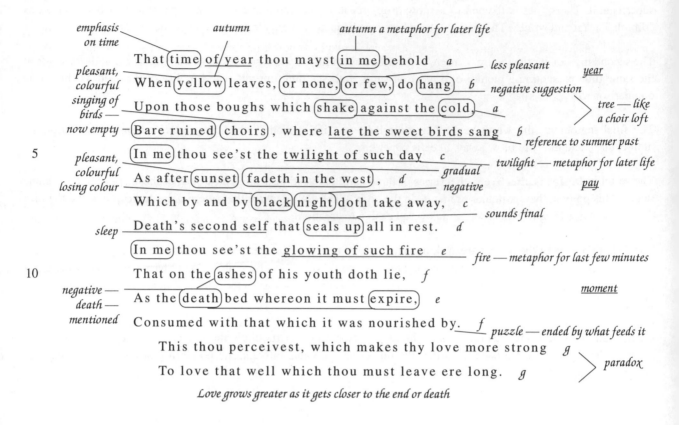

emphasis on time — autumn — autumn a metaphor for later life

That (time) of/year thou mayst (in me) behold   *a* — less pleasant   *year*

pleasant, colourful — When (yellow) leaves, (or none,) (or few,) do (hang)   *b* — negative suggestion

singing of birds — Upon those boughs which (shake) against the (cold,)   *a*   tree — like a choir loft

now empty — (Bare ruined) (choirs), where late the sweet birds sang   *b* — reference to summer past

5   pleasant, colourful — (In me) thou see'st the twilight of such day   *c* — twilight — metaphor for later life

losing colour — As after (sunset) (fadeth in the west),   *d*   gradual negative   *pay*

Which by and by (black)(night) doth take away,   *c* — sounds final

sleep — Death's second self that (seals up) all in rest.   *d*

(In me) thou see'st the glowing of such fire   *e* — fire — metaphor for last few minutes

10   That on the (ashes) of his youth doth lie,   *f*   *moment*

negative — death — mentioned — As the (death) bed whereon it must (expire,)   *e*

Consumed with that which it was nourished by.   *f* — puzzle — ended by what feeds it

This thou perceivest, which makes thy love more strong   *g*   paradox

To love that well which thou must leave ere long.   *g*

Love grows greater as it gets closer to the end or death

Main techniques — Why does the poet use a sonnet form?

    Structure — *Shakespearean sonnet — three rhyming quatrains which are connected by time reflected "in me"*
        each quatrain deals with shorter period of time: year → day → moment
        final couplet has paradox.

    Word choice — *images —*
        have increasing negative, bleak connotations — autumn has some colour — remembers summer; twilight
        has fading colour — sleep like death; fire has only glowing colour — death mentioned particularly.

Ideas — *The increasing love for something about to be lost;*
    the value of life increases as death threatens.

The speaker in this Shakespearean sonnet is a lover thinking about death and addressing his love. He is saying that his growing old makes love even stronger. A feeling of sadness is conveyed to the speaker's love and to the reader. The rhyme-scheme and the punctuation suggest that the sonnet has three quatrains and a couplet. The quatrains are related because "thou" is addressed in each one and because all of them deal with the idea introduced by the first two words of the poem, "that time". Each quatrain is a metaphor which relates a shorter period and a longer period to the span of the poet's life: Autumn is to the year; twilight is to the day; the final glowing is to the fire as the present is to the poet's whole life. The final couplet tells of the consequence of this thought.

The quatrains are not only related, but also develop the idea of time. The span of the successive metaphors becomes shorter and shorter — the first deals with the year, the second with the day, and the third with the few minutes during which a fire flickers before it dies. In the successive quatrains, there is increased emphasis upon what lies ahead. The first does not look forward at all: it looks back at the disappearing summer. The second looks forward to the black night "by and by", and the third to the time, a few moments away, when the flickering fire will die. This development is related to a third progression: a movement toward consideration of that which is at the heart of the poet's sadness, the approach of death.

In the first quatrain, death is only implied by the connotations of such words as "hang", "shake", and "cold". In the second, reference to "black night" connotes death, and the word "death". is actually used; but its use in "death's second self, that seals up all in rest" is a figurative reference not to death but to sleep. The third contains a series of words which figuratively stand for death itself: "ashes", "death-bed", and "consumed". As life fades, there is deterioration of the senses which suggests death - the coming of coldness and silence in the first quatrain, darkness in the second, coldness and darkness in the third.

The third quatrain expresses an element not developed in the earlier quatrains — a paradox: the fire is "consumed", says the poet, "with that which it was nourished by". In other words, that which nurtured life was also that which brought death closer. There is a similar paradox in the couplet: the love of the person addressed grows stronger at the instant the speaker in the poem, who inspires that very love, approaches death.

In the final couplet, the speaker — previously the subject of the quatrains — becomes the secondary figure. "Thou" becomes a central figure. The poet says, "To love that well which thou must leave ere long". The poet, imaginatively looking to death, represents himself with two inanimate pronouns, "that" and "which". This is the most impressive suggestion of death in the poem and it ends the sonnet with a climax for which everything before has been a gradual preparation. The analysis of the figurative language in this poem makes a vital contribution to an understanding of the thought and feeling of the sonnet.

CHAPTER 5

Examples of Textual Analysis from Past Higher Papers

BOY AT THE WINDOW

Seeing the snowman standing all alone
In dusk and cold is more than he can bear.
The small boy weeps to hear the wind prepare
A night of gnashings and enormous moan.
His tearful sight can hardly reach to where
The pale-faced figure with bitumen eyes
Returns him such a god-forsaken stare
As outcast Adam gave to Paradise.

The man of snow is, nonetheless, content,
Having no wish to go inside and die.
Still, he is moved to see the youngster cry.
Though frozen water is his element,
He melts enough to drop from one soft eye
A trickle of the purest rain, a tear
For the child at the bright pane surrounded by
Such warmth, such light, and so much fear.

Richard Wilbur

Understanding and Analysis

(a)   There are two stanzas in this poem. How does the title of the poem relate to the different viewpoint in each stanza?   **2**

(b)   (i)   What feelings does the boy experience in stanza one (lines 1–8)?   **2**

  (ii)   Explain, by close reference to the language and/or other features of stanza one, how the poet makes you aware of these feelings.   **4**

(c)   The poet refers to Adam and to Paradise (line 8). How can you relate these to
  (i)   the situation of the boy   and   (ii)   the situation of the snowman?   **4**

(d)   Explain, by close reference to the language of stanza 2, how the poet makes you aware of the snowman's feelings.   **4**

(e)   Comment fully on the positioning of "nonetheless" (line 9) and "Still" (line 11).   **4**

Evaluation

(f)
  "... a tear
  For the child at the bright pane surrounded by
  Such warmth, such light, such love, and so much fear."

  Look again at the poem as a whole and comment fully on the extent to which these lines seem a satisfying conclusion, both in terms of the poem's ideas and the poem's structure.   **10**

  (30)

ONE ART

The art of losing isn't hard to master;
so many things seem filled with the intent
to be lost that their loss is no disaster.

Lose something every day. Accept the fluster
5   of lost door keys, the hour badly spent.
The art of losing isn't hard to master.

Then practise losing farther, losing faster:
places, and names, and where it was you meant
to travel. None of these will bring disaster.

10   I lost my mother's watch. And look! my last, or
next-to-last, of three loved houses went.
The art of losing isn't hard to master.

I lost two cities, lovely ones. And, vaster,
15   some realms I owned, two rivers, a continent.
I miss them, but it wasn't a disaster.

— Even losing you (the joking voice, a gesture
I love) I shan't have lied. It's evident.
The art of losing's not too hard to master,
20   Though it may look like (*Write* it!) like disaster.

Elizabeth Bishop

Understanding and Analysis

(a)   Comment on two of the ways in which the losses in the first stanza are made to seem unimportant.   **2**

(b)   At the beginning of the poem, the poet seems sure of herself and almost light-hearted. Explain how any three of the following help to give that impression in lines 4–9:

     (i)   word choice
     (ii)   sentence structure
     (iii)   rhyme
     (iv)   rhythm
     (v)   point of view
     (vi)   sound.   **6**

(c)   (i)   Explain how each of these losses might have personal significance:

             "I lost my mother's watch" (line 10);
             "my last . . . of three loved houses" (lines 10 and 11);
             "I lost two cities" (line 14).   **6**

     (ii)   "Some realms I owned, two rivers, a continent" (line 15)

            Suggest the ways in which these things might be regarded as "lost".   **2**

     (iii)   "— Even losing you . . ." (line 17)

            What devices are used to draw your attention to the importance of the loss in the last stanza?   **2**

(d)   What significance can you see in the change of the first line of the poem in the last verse:

          "The art of losing's not too hard to master," (line 19)?   **2**

Evaluation

(e)   (i)   "The art of losing's not too hard to master
             Though it may look like (*Write* it!) like disaster." (lines 19 and 20)

         These lines are a variation of the first stanza and they are echoed elsewhere in the poem. Explain fully what you think these lines mean.

     (ii)   You should then go on to consider how your understanding of the whole poem may have deepened after close study of these lines. You may wish also to consider the overall rhyme scheme and form of the poem in reaching your conclusions.   **10**

(30)

SONNET 65

Since brass, nor stone, nor earth, nor boundless sea,
But sad mortality o'ersways their power,
How with this rage shall beauty hold a plea,
Whose action is no stronger than a flower?
5   O, how shall summer's honey breath hold out
Against the wrackful siege of battering days,
When rocks impregnable are not so stout,
Nor gates of steel so strong, but Time decays?
O fearful meditation! Where, alack,
10   Shall Time's best jewel from Time's chest lie hid?
Or what strong hand can hold his swift foot back?
Or who his spoil of beauty can forbid?
     O, none, unless this miracle have might,
     That in black ink my love may still shine bright.

Shakespeare

Understanding and Analysis

(a)   (i)   Suggest a reason why one of the items mentioned in the first line might have been selected to
                illustrate the point that is being made in lines 1 and 2.   **2**

        (ii)   What rhythm can you identify in the first line?   **2**

        (iii) Explain fully in your own words the contrast which is set out in lines 1–4.   **4**

(b)   (i)   Explain the personification in line 5.   **2**

        (ii)   Go on to explain how effective you find the imagery in lines 5–8 in establishing a similar
                contrast to the one in lines 1–4.   **4**

(c)   Show how the use of questions in the poem helps you to appreciate the developing mood or feelings
        in the poem.   **4**

(d)   What do you think the poet means by "fearful meditation" (line 8)?   **2**

Evaluation

(e)   Explain how satisfying you find the paradox or puzzle in the final lines (13 and 14) in form and
        content as a resolution or an answer to the poet's fear or "fearful meditation" expressed throughout
        the sonnet?

        In your answer you should take this opportunity to consider the ideas and techniques of the poem as
        a whole, although you may be concentrating particularly on the final lines.   **10**

                                                                                                                     (30)

young, innocent, unaware

BOY AT THE WINDOW < two perspectives — inside → out; outside → in

Boy looking out of window   loneliness

Seeing the snowman standing all (alone) *a*

negative —   In dusk and (cold) is more than he can (bear.) *b*   emotive words — boy is
                                                                                      full of sorrow for
very young gets   The (small) boy (weeps) to hear the wind prepare *b*   snowman
our sympathy

A night of gnashings and enormous moan. *a*   sound — of wind

5   His (tearful) sight can hardly reach to where *b*

white — but   The (pale-faced) figure with (bitumen) eyes *c*   stone — cold, unfeeling
not alive
                                                                                  negative connotation —
                           Returns him such a ((god)-forsaken) stare *b*   desolation

like snowman   < As outcast Adam gave to Paradise. (Adam/Eve story) *c*   religious connotation
outside

looking in at a boy standing at window

                                                                                position in middle of
The man of snow is, nonetheless, content, *d*   sentence — emphasises
                                                                                snowman's contentment

10   Having no wish to go inside and die. *e* > paradox — would melt — die — in heat

position — two   < (Still,) he is (moved) to see the youngster cry. *e*
meanings:
motionless, yet   Though frozen water is his (element,) *d*   he is made of water (tears)

                           He melts enough to drop from one (soft) eye *e*   sympathy

positive —   A trickle of the (purest) rain, a tear (*b*)
innocence

15   For the child at the (bright) pane surrounded by *e*   positive connotations of
                                                                                  home — warmth/cosiness
                           Such (warmth,) such (light,) and (so much fear). *b*   rhythm of final line
                                                                                  — oxymoron is shocking —
                                                                                  warmth / light and fear
                     repetition   dramatic contrast in last three words
                           "fear" comes as a startling final word

Main techniques — Think about word choice, contrast and structure.

    Word choice —   emotive words for boy — weep, bear, tearful
                     sound of words — gnashing/moan
                     oxymorons to emphasise contrast — still/moved; warmth and light/fear
                     words that gain our sympathy for both boy and snowman.
    Contrast   >   perspectives of boy and snowman
                >   outside/inside — cosy world of home; fearful world of wind/snow
                >   feeling/unfeeling
    Structure   —   develops the contrast between the boy's perspective (first half of the poem) and the snowman's
                     (second half).

Ideas   —   Both sadness and pity for each other.
              They stand on opposite sides of the window.
              Window perhaps represents division between those who know about good and evil and those who don't
              (Adam before he was cast out of Paradise).

The final two lines of *Boy at the Window* are an effective conclusion to the poem because the unusual combination of "warmth" and "light" with "fear" forces the reader to look again at the ideas expressed in each part of the poem. The form and the title of "Boy at the Window" also lead us to compare two different perspectives. The title suggests that a boy is at a window looking out and this is the point of view of the first stanza. The title could also suggest that an outsider is observing a boy standing at a window and this is the perspective of the second stanza as the snowman observes the boy.

The boy pities the snowman who lives in loneliness, darkness and cold. The personification of the wind suggests extreme sorrow and pain with the connotations of words like "gnashing" and the sense and sound of "enormous moan". Words like "pale-faced" and "god-forsaken" and the allusion to the Garden of Eden when Adam was cast out suggests that this is a world where evil and unhappiness reign. The knowledge of sin and evil characterise this "outside" world. It is cold and lacking in human warmth.

Yet the snowman finds reason to pity the boy who, from the snowman's point of view, is suffocated in a bright heat of childish innocence. The ambiguity of the word "still" draws attention to that line suggesting that "yet" the snowman — even in his outcast state — can feel sorrow for the boy. It also draws attention to the physical stillness of the snowman contrasted to "moved" in feelings. Sorrow and pain is part of the lot of those on the outside with the snowman. Significantly, the words "soft" and "purest" imply innocence and vulnerability, a stark contrast to the word "god-forsaken" used in the first stanza to describe the outside world.

The final line emphasises the boy's situation with its rhythmic monosyllables and repetition of "such": "Such warmth, such light, and so much fear". The juxtaposition of warmth and light with "fear" and the position of this word at the very end of the poem rhyming with the previous two lines is dramatic and leaves us reflecting on the condition of both boy and snowman and on their reflections on each other.

There is much left unsaid in this poem which makes the variety of interpretation all the richer. To me, the poet is suggesting that the difference between the two worlds is in the knowledge of good and evil; the window is the barrier between the two. The boy is young and innocent and therefore fears what he does not know or understand: the horror and pain of sin, loneliness and even death. The "snowman" — or any man who realises this fallen state of man — is no longer frightened but perhaps hardened and unable to return to the bright world of warmth and innocence. Perhaps he even weeps for the innocent who await disillusionment — and which the innocent might already suspect, instinctively, is lurking. This is a poem provoking reflection, which is not cheerful, on the human condition.

ONE ART

What is it?
Losing?
Mastering art of losing?
Writing?

skill — *vague* — *colloquial*

The art of losing isn't hard to master; *a*

exaggerated number — so many things seem filled with the intent *b*

to be lost that their loss is no disaster. *a*

no subject informal — *indefinite* — *frequency* — *no subject* — *definite*

① Lose something every day. Accept the fluster *a*

5 of lost door keys, the hour badly spent. *b* ② *time*

repetition first line — The art of losing isn't hard to master. *a*

sound — repetition

Then practise losing farther, losing faster: *a*

polysyndetic makes list seem endless — places, and names, and where it was you meant *b* — *memories*

to travel. None of these will bring disaster. *a*

definite *two meanings?*

10 *becomes personal* — I lost my mother's watch. And look! my last, or *a* — *emotion*

next-to-last, of three loved houses went. *b* — *feminine rhyme light/humorous*

first line — The art of losing isn't hard to master. *a* *homes?*

a strange loss

suggests kingship — I lost two cities, lovely ones. And, vaster, *a* — *all feminine rhymes*

15 some realms I owned, two rivers, a continent. *b* — *huge losses — exaggerated*

I miss them, but it wasn't a disaster. *a*

this loss most important *repetitious — but slight change* *parentheses make voice and gesture seem like after-thoughts*

abrupt break — —Even losing you (the joking voice, a gesture *a*

I love) I shan't have lied. It's evident. *b*

colloquial — casual language — The art of losing's not too hard to master, *a* — *not quite like first line — seems more like a disaster perhaps*

20 Though it may look like (Write it!) like disaster. *a*

change — weaker *parentheses emphasise determination*

Main Techniques — *Consider as many techniques as you can — structure, word choice, symbolism, rhyme/rhythm, tone — even punctuation. How is each used to suggest superficial control and inner turmoil?*

Structure — villanelle — very tight rhyme scheme

Images / symbolism — representing greater losses than initially suggested

Tone — casual — use of colloquial language

rhyme (feminine — two syllable) sounds light-hearted

move from general beginning to increasingly personal

Punctuation — dash — emphasises change in final four-line stanza — to very personal reinforced by words in parentheses.

Ideas — *Techniques suggest that superficially the ideas are humorous / light-hearted but the form and tightness of the poem suggest that poet is trying to contain emotions.*

The first line of *One Art* is deceptively simple and light-hearted. The number of items ("so many"), their apparent unimportance ("things"), and the use of the passive voice ("seemed filled with the intent") suggest that losing things is a common daily occurrence which does not deserve much consideration. This is confirmed by the final phrase in this stanza, "their loss is no disaster". The colloquial language and the off-hand manner ("lose something", "accept the fluster") further convinces us that there is no disaster in losing.

The pace of the poem increases in the third stanza with the attractive-sounding phrase, "losing further, losing faster" and the numerous and various items connected by "and". The lost items seem increasingly important or valuable: car keys to place names to "my mother's watch". The items seem a bit absurd when houses, cities and realms (which suggest kingships) are listed, but by this point we realise that we are not to take these items literally; they are representative of something even more significant than the item itself — perhaps relationships. My mother's "watch" could have two meanings; houses could mean homes or family arrangements. By this stage the poet's insistence that the losing isn't hard to master and it isn't a disaster becomes less convincing. She seems to be protesting too much and there is a sense that she is laughing lightly to hide the real intensity of her true feelings.

The final stanza of the poem strongly suggests this serious aspect. It is set off from the others by a dash — an abrupt break — indicating a significant change. Everything about these final four lines suggests now the value of the subject matter and the persona's restraint in containing her emotion. The words themselves are touching: "the joking voice" and "a gesture I love" in parentheses as if this is unimportant extra information that could be omitted. The familiar refrain changes here: now the art of losing's not "too hard" to master. In a second parenthesis the poet seems to be forcing herself to write — with an exclamation — the word "disaster".

The overall form of the poem, the very tightly structured villanelle, convinced me that the persona in the poem was exercising great restraint in trying to keep her emotions in check. She was determined to deny that any loss, any attachment — "(even you)" — could possibly mean anything or be a disaster. The feminine rhyme throughout deceptively leads us to read the stanzas quickly and to think that this subject is a light-hearted exploration of little importance. The title also gains in significance by the end of the poem: is this one art among many or is this *the* one art?

"Deceptive" is the word for this poem. It reads quickly and lightly. Only the careful reader will have recognised that the poet / persona is on the brink of tears here and that the loss has been almost too great to bear — without writing perhaps and maybe that is the "one art".

SONNET 65

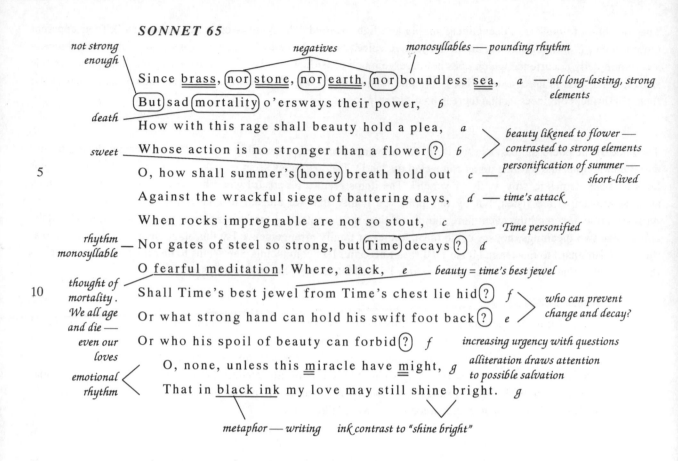

Annotations on the poem:

- not strong enough
- negatives
- monosyllables — pounding rhythm

Since **brass**, (nor) **stone**, (nor) **earth**, (nor) boundless **sea**, *a* — all long-lasting, strong elements

(But) sad (mortality) o'ersways their power, *b*

death
How with this rage shall beauty hold a plea, *a*

sweet
Whose action is no stronger than a flower(?) *b* — beauty likened to flower — contrasted to strong elements

5 O, how shall summer's (honey) breath hold out *c* — personification of summer — short-lived

Against the wrackful siege of battering days, *d* — time's attack

When rocks impregnable are not so stout, *c*

rhythm monosyllable
Nor gates of steel so strong, but (Time) decays(?) *d* — Time personified

O fearful meditation! Where, alack, *e* — beauty = time's best jewel

thought of mortality. We all age and die —
10 Shall Time's best jewel from Time's chest lie hid(?) *f*

Or what strong hand can hold his swift foot back(?) *e* — who can prevent change and decay?

even our loves
Or who his spoil of beauty can forbid(?) *f* — increasing urgency with questions

emotional rhythm
O, none, unless this **m**iracle have **m**ight, *g* — alliteration draws attention to possible salvation

That in **black ink** my love may still shine bright. *g*

metaphor — writing   ink contrast to "shine bright"

Main techniques — Consider as many techniques as you can — structure, imagery, symbolism, punctuation, rhyme, rhythm. How is each used to suggest the brevity of man's life?

Structure — sonnet — three rhyming quatrains with each quatrain focusing on conflict between strength and weakness — between time and beauty
final couplet considers possible solution — writing

Punctuation — increasing number of questions and exclamations emphasises emotional nature of problem

Rhythm — strong pounding rhythm through poem emphasises the relentlessness of time's attack on beauty. Stems from use of monosyllables

Symbols — jewel — beauty; black ink — writing; personification of time.

Ideas — There is nowhere for beauty to hide from relentless attack by time. Only in writing — in poetry — can beauty and love be preserved for time changes appearance of all nature — even the strongest elements.

Shakespeare is writing in this sonnet about the harshness of time which is personified throughout the sonnet. The only hope of gaining any immortality is through verses — "black ink". Each of the quatrains develops the conflict between time and the victim of time — love and beauty.

The first stanza says that there is no object, not even brass, stone, earth or sea (strong elemental forces), that can escape destruction. The speaker then asks how beauty which is as frail and short-lived as a flower can escape. The repetition of the negative "nor" with the other monosyllables of the first line draws attention to the relentless attack on beauty over time.

The second stanza also questions how the beauty of summer, its "honey breath", can withstand the battering forces of winter. The imagery of battle with words like "wrackful siege", "impregnable" and "stout" shows the intense conflict between beauty and destructive forces.

The third quatrain begins with the emotional exclamation of this frightening thought — nothing can outlast time. If this is true, where can "Time's best jewel" be hid? This image suggests the value and beauty of love and the horror of the realisation that there is nowhere to hide from the ravages of the years. The rhythm of the final line of this quatrain with its steady pounding of monosyllables continues to remind us of the relentless battering that mortality must face.

The increasing number of questions and exclamations in the final lines as well as this relentless pounding rhythm conveys the developing urgency and concern of the speaker that all is lost and that Time is truly the victor in this battle with Life. However, the final rhyming couplet suggests that there is a solution to be found in verses, in poetry. The image of "black ink" contrasting with the brightness of love suggests a type of permanence in which man can find some consolation. The negative words in this couplet, "none" and "unless", suggest the tentativeness of this suggestion; nevertheless, the continuing use of the rhythm and the resounding rhyme in the couplet furthers a conclusion in which the reader is meant to take, at least superficially, some consolation.

This is a poem which benefits from being read aloud. The tone of measured solemnity at the beginning of the poem continues into the second quatrain where the sound of "rocks impregnable", "not so stout" and "steel so strong" sound like the blows delivered by Time's hammer. The sound is echoed again in the third stanza with "what strong hand" and "swift foot back". The final couplet confirms the force against which all men must struggle. The speaker (or writer is perhaps more appropriate) is any lover who is saddened and even threatened by the sense of "sad mortality" when contemplating his love's beauty.

CHAPTER 6

Further Practice in Textual Analysis

Their Lonely Betters is a poem, like those in Chapter 1, which makes comparisons between the natural world — birds and flowers — and the world of man.

Annotate the poem, noting particularly the contrasts or differences between the two worlds. Are there any similarities as well? Consider particularly the final stanza. After you have taken notes on word choice, rhyme, rhythm, sound, the title and final lines, try answering the question for evaluation.

Then look at the questions for analysis to see which techniques or aspects you may have omitted to consider in your own analysis of the poem.

THEIR LONELY BETTERS

As I listened from a beach-chair in the shade
To all the noises that my garden made,
It seemed only proper that words
Should be withheld from vegetables and birds.

5   A robin with no Christian name ran through
A Robin-Anthem which was all it knew,
And rustling flowers for some third party waited
To say which pairs, if any, should get mated.

No one of them was capable of lying,
10   There was not one which knew that it was dying
Or could have with a rhythm or a rhyme
Assumed responsibility for time.

Let them leave language to their lonely betters
Who count some days and long for certain letters;
15   We, too, make noises when we laugh or weep;
Words are for those with promises to keep.

W.H. Auden

Evaluation

(a)   The title *Their Lonely Betters* is repeated in the final stanza. In the light of the whole poem and with particular reference to the last four lines, say what you understand by "their lonely betters".   **10**

Understanding and Analysis

(b)   (i)   What is the situation and the mood suggested in the opening stanza (lines 1–4)?   **2**

(ii)   How do any two of the following in the first stanza (lines 1–4) help the reader to respond to the mood of the narrator:
(1) rhyme; (2) rhythm; (3) word choice; (4) sentence structure; (5) sound; (6) tone?   **4**

(c)   Trace the ways in which the distinction between "noises" (line 2) and "words" (line 3) is continued and developed in the remainder of the poem.   **6**

(d)   Comment in detail on the ways in which the poet makes us aware of the differences between human existence and the life of his garden in the second stanza (lines 5–8).   **4**

(e)   Within the context of lines 9–12, comment on the different possible interpretations of the expression "responsibility for time" (line 12).   **4**

(30)

Grey Squirrel is in some ways like the poems of Chapter 1: it makes a comparison between man and animal behaviour. It is also like some of the poems in Chapter 2 in which the persona of the poem is important. The tone of the poem, like those in Chapter 3, is a key to understanding the ideas.

Think about the encounter between the squirrel and the persona of the poem. What comparisons is the poet making between the two?

Annotate the poem, considering especially techniques such as word choice, imagery and tone. Think particularly about the difficult parts of the poem: "the keen teeth of winter" and "what conscience is to the survivor". Then answer the evaluation question on the next page.

Go on to look at the questions for analysis and note any aspects you might have considered in your critical evaluation.

GREY SQUIRREL

Accused by my interest, you start —
squirreling to your feet — and let fall
the evidence, in a chestnut shell.
You place both hands upon your heart
5   as if to say I've got the wrong guy.
Take it easy, I too have survived —
therefore guilty.

And know the Fall, a hasty scarper
among the dying and the discarded
10   for what's to be hidden and hoarded.
What's to keep the keen teeth of winter
from meeting in my throat? I'm aware
of what conscience is to the survivor —
something to hide.

15   So I'm studying you, to discover
how to freeze, become an illustration
in a book thought suitable for children
before bewildering my own tall accuser
with the smokescreen of my tail as I flee
20   — no doubt up one of those open-mouthed trees
with raised eyebrows.

Brian McCabe

Understanding and Analysis

(a)   Look carefully at stanza one (lines 1–7).

    (i)   What encounter takes place in the first stanza?   **1**

    (ii)   What imaginary encounter is suggested to the narrator by this real encounter?   **1**

    (iii)   Trace in detail the ways in which the idea of an accusation is developed in lines 1–5.   **4**

    (iv)   Comment on the language and tone of "Take it easy" (line 6).   **2**

    (v)   How does line 6 introduce a new relationship between the man and the squirrel?   **2**

    (vi)   In what ways does the author draw attention to "therefore guilty" (line 7)? What effect does the positioning of this expression have on the meaning of stanza one (lines 1–7)?   **4**

(b)   (i)   The word "Fall" in line 8 might refer to the autumn or to the religious idea of mankind's fall from innocence. How is each of these possible meanings developed in stanza two (lines 8–14)?   **4**

    (ii)   "What's to keep the keen teeth of winter
                from meeting in my throat?"
    In what ways is the image contained in these lines central to the poem?   **2**

Evaluation

(c)   By looking closely at the imagery and tone of the poem and in the final stanza (lines 15–21) in particular, show what the poet has, in the end, learned from studying the squirrel.   **10**

                                                        (30)

This poem, a modern ballad by E.E. Cummings, is unusual. The form of the poem is important to consider. Traditional ballads tell a story, use repetition, rely on sensual detail (particularly colour) and sound.

Read the poem and try "to crack" the tale. What is the story? Annotate the poem paying particular attention to features characteristic of the ballad. When you have noted the repetition, you should consider slight changes or alterations as well. What significance do you see in the changes in this ballad?

Answer the evaluation question first. Then do the questions for analysis.

ALL IN GREEN WENT MY LOVE RIDING

All in green went my love riding
on a great horse of gold
into the silver dawn.

four lean hounds crouched low and smiling
5   the merry deer ran before.

Fleeter be they than dappled dreams
the swift sweet deer
the red rare deer.

Four red roebuck at a white water
10   the cruel bugle sang before.

Horn at hip went my love riding
riding the echo down
into the silver dawn.

four lean hounds crouched low and smiling
15   the level meadows ran before.

Softer be they than slippered sleep
the lean lithe deer
the fleet flown deer.

Four fleet does at a gold valley
20   the famished arrow sang before.

Bow at belt went my love riding
riding the mountain down
into the silver dawn.

four lean hounds crouched low and smiling
25   the sheer peaks ran before.

Paler be they than daunting death
the sleek slim deer
the tall tense deer.

Four tall stags at a green mountain
30   the lucky hunter sang before.

All in greeen went my love riding
on a great horse of gold
into the silver dawn.

four lean hounds crouched low and smiling
35   my heart fell dead before.

E.E. Cummings

Evaluation

(a)   The couplet has been repeated throughout the poem with minor variations. What does the variation in the final couplet of the poem have on your appreciation of the situation and your enjoyment of the poem? In your answer you should consider the repetition and variations in the poem as a whole. You should consider how other aspects are repeated and varied such as sound, verse form, use of adjectives and verbs, colour and images.   **10**

Understanding and Analysis

(b)   What do the word choice and the sentence structure in the first three lines suggest to you about the setting and time of the poem?   **2**

(c)   Comment fully on words in line four which you think convey tone or atmosphere through their connotations or implications.   **4**

(d)   Sound and imagery are important in ballads. Comment on the way in which each of these is used to good effect at one place in the poem.   **4**

(e)   Traditional ballads are characterised by the use of:
   (i)   vivid colour;
   (ii)   repetition;
   (iii) simple words.
   Show how an example of each of these features helps to make the poem more memorable to you.   **6**

(f)   Both the beauty and the vulnerability of the deer are depicted in this ballad. Show how effective you find examples of either word choice or imagery in conveying these characteristics of the deer.   **4**

(30)

Opera is a poem similar to those in Chapter 2. It is about a family relationship.

Think about the persona of the poem. Who do you imagine is speaking? What kind of relationship is being described? Annotate the poem, paying particular attention to words which seem unusual or out of place, such as "stagey chandeliers", the title and the final line "wearing her songs".

Write a critical evaluation of the poem saying what the poem means to you. Consider two or three main techniques which were important in terms of your understanding of the poem's ideas, such as the persona of the poem, the word choice and the imagery.

OPERA

Throw all your stagey chandeliers in wheelbarrows and move
      them north
To celebrate my mother's sewing-machine
And her beneath an eighty-watt bulb, pedalling
5   Iambs on an antique metal footplate
Powering the needle through its regular lines,
Doing her work. To me as a young boy
That was her typewriter. I'd watch
Her hands and feet in unison, or read
10   Between her calves the wrought-iron letters:
SINGER. Mass-produced polished wood and metal,
It was a powerful instrument. I stared
Hard at its brilliant needle's eye that purred
And shone at night; and then each morning after
15   I went to work at school, wearing her songs.

Robert Crawford

GLOSSARY

alliteration	The repetition of the same consonant sound at the beginning of words, e.g. "black bull" in *Revelation*.
allusion	A reference to another event, place, person, or piece of literature, e.g. Adam and Eve in *Boy at the Window*.
ambiguity	Words or phrases in which the meaning is unclear or which has more than one possible interpretation, e.g. *Boy Driving His Father to Confession*.
archaic	Old-fashioned; used to describe words which are seldom used any more, e.g. "this Thou perceivest" in the Shakespearean *Sonnet 73*.
assonance	The repetition of similar vowel sounds, e.g. "too blue" and "goes down" in *The Way My Mother Speaks*.
blank verse	Unrhymed poetry in iambic pentameter.
cliché	A phrase, idea or image that has been used so much that it has lost its original meaning and significance, e.g. "hot on their heels" or "hit the media" in *Alba Einstein*.
climax	Building up to a high point or important moment.
colloquial	Ordinary, everyday speech, e.g. "became peak-viewing" or "Top speed's their only one".
connotation	The implication or suggestion attached to a word or phrase.
couplet	Two consecutive lines of verse that rhyme, e.g. the final lines of a Shakespearean sonnet.
dialect	A way of speaking in a certain area of the country, e.g. "what like is it?" or "hurled awa".
enjambement	A line of verse that flows on to the next line without pause; a run-on line; see *Sandpiper*.
euphemism	A softer, less harsh way of expressing something unpleasant, e.g. "passing away" instead of "death".
extended image	A comparison that is repeated in more than one place in a poem or is continued throughout the writing; see the Shakespearean sonnets.
feminine rhyme	Rhyme of more than one syllable, e.g. "constitution" and "destitution"; "master" and "disaster" in the poem *One Art*.
figurative language	Language which is symbolic or metaphorical; not meant to be taken literally, such as similes, metaphors and personification.
hyperbole	Elaborate exaggeration, e.g. "I lost two cities" in *One Art*.

imagery	The use of words to create pictures or images for the reader.
infinitive	"To" plus a verb form, such as "to jump" or "to swim".
internal rhyme	Rhyming words within a line rather than at the end of lines.
inversion	Word order which places the verb before the subject or otherwise "inverts" the usual structure of a sentence with which we are familiar — subject, verb, object — and thereby puts emphasis on the word which is out of order, e.g. "Great is the battle god" or "Blushing, she fled".
irony	Saying one thing while meaning another; a word or phrase has a surface meaning but the opposite, often contradictory, meaning is implied e.g. *War Is Kind*.
jargon	Language which is particular to a particular profession or occupation, "A.E. Fun Park" or "glottal stop".
juxtaposition	Placing together two items which are not usually not placed together; a striking combination, e.g. "bright splendid shroud" in *War is Kind*.
masculine rhyme	Rhyme of one syllable, e.g. "might" and "bright".
metaphor	A comparison of two things to make a description more vivid. The metaphor states that one thing is the other; whereas, a simile would say that it is "like" or "as" the other object.
metre	Regular use of stressed and unstressed syllables in poetry.
monosyllabic	Single syllable.
mood	The overall emotional feeling or atmosphere communicated by a piece of writing.
octave	The first eight lines of a Petrarchan sonnet, e.g. *Design*.
onomatopoeia	The use of words whose sound copies the sound of the thing they describe, e.g. "bang", "hiss" or "splash".
oxymoron	A figure of speech which joins together words of opposite meanings, e.g. "controlled panic" in *Sandpiper*.
paradox	A puzzle; a statement that appears contradictory, but when it is considered more closely it is seen to be true, e.g. "Consumed with that which it was nourished by" in *Sonnet 73*.
parallel sentence structure	Two sentences follow the same structure of syntax or pattern. Usually used to show either a contrast in the ideas of the two sentences or a similarity; also referred to as balanced sentences. See *An Irish Airman Foresees His Death*.

parenthetical	From parenthesis; a word or phrase which gives extra information and is not strictly speaking necessary for the sense. These phrases are placed within brackets or commas.
parody	A work that is written in imitation of another work, usually written to make fun of the original work.
pejorative	A negative suggestion or implication of a word.
pentameter	A line of verse containing five feet.
persona	The "person" in the poem — not necessarily the poet; it is the perspective or point of view from which the poem is written.
personification	Giving human qualities to an inanimate object. A metaphor in which an inanimate object is likened to a person, e.g. "the keen teeth of winter" in *Grey Squirrel*.
polysyllabic	Made up of more than one syllable.
polysyndetic	The joining of words in a list with "and" between each of the items. Usually this is used to emphasise or draw attention to some feature of the list, e.g. "minute and vast and clear".
pun	A play on words; two words that have similar sounds but different meanings, e.g. "sole" and "soul".
quatrain	A stanza of four lines which rhyme; see the Shakespearean sonnets.
refrain	Repetition throughout a poem of a phrase, line or verse.
rhetorical question	A question which does not require an answer because the answer is obvious or because it is implied in the question.
rhyme	Corresponding sounds in words, usually at the end of lines.
rhyme scheme	The pattern of rhyme in a poem.
sarcasm	(From the Greek meaning "tearing flesh"). Usually a very cruel or cutting remark.
satire	The exposing of human failings by ridiculing them.
sestet	The last six lines of a Petrarchan sonnet, e.g. *Design*.
sibilants	Words which begin with "s" or soft "c", like "soft shoes".
simile	A comparison of one thing to another in order to make a description more vivid. Similes use the words "like" or "as" to make the comparison, e.g. "the beach hisses like fat".
simple sentence	A sentence which has one clause with a subject and a verb.
sonnet	A fourteen-line poem. A Petrarchan sonnet has an octave (eight lines) and a sestet (six lines) which is often a puzzle followed by an "answer" or a resolution. A Shakespearean sonnet is three quatrains plus a couplet. The quatrains are often related and an idea is developed throughout the quatrains reaching a climax or conclusion in the final couplet.

stanza	The blocks of lines into which a poem is divided.
stream of consciousness	A technique in which the writer writes down thoughts and emotions as they come into mind without seeming to bother about an order or a structure, e.g. *The Way My Mother Speaks*.
structure	The way that a poem has been put together. It might depend upon stanzas, verses, or forms like sonnet or villanelle, or pattern of rhyme or rhythm.
style	The individual way in which a writer uses language to express ideas.
symbol	A physical object representative of something else, like a dove is used to symbolise peace; see the poems *War is Kind* and *One Art*.
syntax	The way in which sentences are constructed.
theme	The central idea or ideas that are explored in a piece of literature.
tone	The author's voice or overall impression created in the poem. It is created in a combination of ways, such as word choice, sentence structure, rhythm, rhyme.
transferred epithet	An adjective which is usually applied to a person is applied to an object to draw attention to the quality, e.g. a prisoner in a "condemned cell".
verse	A unit of poetry.
villanelle	A verse form which is complex and artificial. It has a very tight rhyme scheme: *a b a a b a a b a a b a a b a a b a a*. Certain lines are repeated entirely: line 1 is repeated in lines 6, 12, 18; line 3 is repeated in lines 9, 15 and 19, e.g. the poem *One Art*.

ACKNOWLEDGEMENTS

We are extremely grateful to the following for permission to use copyright material in this book.

Sparrow from 'COLLECTED POEMS'
Reprinted by permission of the Estate of Norman MacCaig and the Publisher, Hogarth Press.

Ringed Plover by the Water's Edge from 'OLD MAPS AND NEW: SELECTED POEMS'
Reprinted by permission of the Estate of Norman MacCaig and the Publisher, Hogarth Press.

One Art and *Sandpiper* from 'THE COMPLETE POEMS 1927–1979' by Elizabeth Bishop.
Copyright © 1979. 1983 by Alice Helen Methfessel. Reprinted by permission of the Publisher, Farrar, Straus & Giroux, Inc.

The Thought-Fox from 'THE HAWK IN THE RAIN'
Reprinted by permission of the Author, Ted Hughes and the Publisher, Faber and Faber Ltd.

Revelation from 'DREAMING FRANKENSTEIN'
Reprinted by permission of the Author, Liz Lochead and the Publisher, Polygon.

Boy Driving His Father to Confession by Seamus Heany
from 'WRITING AND RESPONDING' by Chris Woodhead.

Men and *Men from Boys* from 'SLATTERN'
Reprinted by permission of the Author, Kate Clanchy and the Publisher, Chatto and Windus.

The Way My Mother Speaks from 'THE OTHER COUNTRY 1990' by Carol Ann Duffy.
Reprinted by permission of the Publisher, Anvil Press Poetry.

War Is Kind by Stephen Crane from 'MODERN AMERICAN POETS'
Edited by Robert Di Yanni and published by Random Century.

Fairy Tale from 'SELECTED POEMS 1954–1982'
Reprinted by permission of the Author, John Fuller.

Alba Einstein from 'SCOTTISH ASSEMBLY'
Reprinted by permission of the Author, Robert Crawford and the Publisher, Chatto and Windus.

An Irish Airman Foresees his Death from 'COLLECTED POEMS' by W.B. Yeats

At the Wellhead from 'THE SPIRIT LEVEL'
Reprinted by permission of the Author, Seamus Heaney and the Publisher, Faber and Faber Ltd.

Design from 'THE POETRY OF ROBERT FROST'
Reprinted by permission of the Estate of Robert Frost, the Editor, Edward Connery Latham and the Publisher, Jonathan Cape.

The Boy at the Window from 'NEW AND COLLECTED POEMS'
Reprinted by permission of the Author, Richard Wilbur and the Publisher, Faber and Faber Ltd.

Printed by Bell & Bain Ltd., Glasgow, Scotland.